Table of Contents

Foreword

I had the privilege of serving on the Wesley board of governors during the entire period covered in this book. It was an incredible journey through times of great change. From the very outset, we had a crucial financial situation that had to be resolved, and that was only the first of many obstacles in our path.

Our reward came not just from solving those problems, but from expanding the seminary's vision and discovering new ways for Wesley to be of service to the denomination and local churches.

It was a long process. Our new president, Doug Lewis, inherited a board that was not well informed about seminary matters. It did not meet very often, and the members did not know each other well enough to have the kind of substantive discussions that could lead to important actions. One of his most important contributions was the gradual formation of a group of individuals who would make Wesley a priority in their lives. He sought out those who were dedicated to working together to make exciting things seem possible—and then to make them happen. He encouraged us to update the bylaws, hold retreats with the faculty, meet with other seminary boards, establish a board development committee, and apply for board development grants from Lilly Endowment—all of which contributed to the board's growth and maturity.

One of his effective recruiting methods was the creation of the President's Advisory Council. That group became a source of qualified individuals who had the time and dedication to become board members or to assume other positions of responsibility.

Doug also proposed the idea of forming a Wesley Council made up of members who would pledge $1,000 a year. Our first response was that we did not know anyone we could ask to do that, but we did find them. As it turned out, they not only gave financial assistance but enthusiastic support as well. Social events such as dinners with well-known speakers and local excursions led to the formation of a close-knit group whose s felt a responsibility to each other and to the seminary.

Those who answered the call to serve were made to feel their contributions were necessary and appreciated, and that their talents were valuable. Board meetings became forums where meaningful issues were discussed and members with different perspectives felt comfortable in the expression of those views. There were times when the board had to make an important decision and most members were quite sure what the outcome would be. But after a long and productive discussion, the final decision was quite different—and much the better for it.

Board dinners at the president's home were eagerly anticipated events when spouses and partners could also take part in seminary life. They also gave us the opportunity to recognize members who had made special contributions during that year and those who had completed their terms. We all enjoyed those gatherings.

For me, and I know for others, those years were a time of personal growth that gave us that special joy which comes from achieving goals that are important and hard to reach. The future will bring new challenges for Wesley, but Wesley now has a board that can deal responsibly and creatively with whatever it may face.

As Doug approached his tenth year as president, the board knew that he was being sought by other institutions. We were worried that he might be thinking of moving on, so we made it our job to convince him than that another ten years at Wesley would be even more exciting than the past decade had been. His decision to stay allowed us to make the kind of progress that could only be realized under a president whose leadership had proven worthy of our trust.

When Doug made his decision to retire, the board decided the best way to honor his many contributions would be to make one of his long-time dreams come true—a leadership center where outstanding younger pastors of all denominations could come together, exchange ideas, and learn from each other. The Center's research, publications, and programs would help denominations to address problem issues and also provide support for local churches. We believe the establishment of the leadership center was a fitting culmination to Doug's time at Wesley. Over the past twelve years, the Lewis Center for Church Leadership has exceeded all of our hopes, and we have every reason to expect that it will continue to do so in the future!

Wesley made dramatic progress in many areas under Doug's leadership. Nothing, however, was more important than building a strong and effective board of governors. They provide the foundation upon which a sound and creative theological school now stands.

Selecting David McAllister-Wilson as Doug's successor proved the board's maturity and its commitment to Wesley's mission. It chose a talented and creative president who would keep the seminary focused on the same path to ever-brighter horizons.

Helen Smith

Helen Smith served on the Wesley Seminary Board of Governors from 1978 through 2003. She chaired the first board development committee, which became integral to Wesley's dramatic turnaround. She also served as chair of the board from 1987-1990.

Preface

I was honored to serve as president of Wesley Seminary for twenty years. Almost every one of those joyful days taught me something new. Perhaps the most significant lesson was that institutional leadership is a daily challenge and a learning process which never ends.

I never planned to write this book. The very idea somehow struck me as vain and self-serving. Twelve years after my retirement, however, colleagues and other friends convinced me the story of Wesley's transformation during my tenure could benefit others. So here it is.

I found Wesley in a serious financial predicament when I took office in the summer of 1982. We tightened our belts, recovered, and eventually prospered—but the story does not end there. No institution can expect to solve its immediate problems and thus be done with them for good. It is inevitable that critical issues will stand in the way of seminary presidents and leaders of other worthy endeavors, now and forever.

They will be called upon to use the full range of their talents and experience to navigate shoal waters as yet uncharted. This account of our voyage—the actions we took, the consequences, and the lessons we learned—is therefore offered to them in the spirit of a gift, in the hope that it might be helpful somewhere along the way.

Primarily, this is a personal account of a call, of an odyssey in the company of like minds with similar goals. The reader will come to understand how the parts of a seminary fit together and the role of leadership in uniting the community around a common purpose that will endure in spite of adversity.

Leadership and Change is divided into five chronological phases. Each of them is shaped by events which we examine through the eyes of the leader—what he did or did not do, and how the institution was affected by the outcome. While the book does have numbers and charts, it is presented in story form. Historical records can protect events from receding out of memory, but stories give us the feelings behind those events. They put us into the action while it happens. They let us share the worry, the hope, the courage, the faith and the laughs that are the fabric of our lives. Stories help us make sense of our place in the flow of time.

This book is not fiction. The people are real, and they made vital contributions to the seminary's recovery and advancement. I am proud of and grateful to each and every one.

Wesley officials graciously provided access to many resources used in this work. They also encouraged the project and helped bring it to fruition. I nevertheless wish to assert this book is a voluntary effort entirely of my own making, and I am solely responsible for its contents.

There are others, not named, who supported this project and made it viable. I will convey my gratitude to them privately.

I dedicate this book to Shirley Savage Lewis, my life partner and wife for sixty years. Most of her contributions to Wesley Seminary and to me remain untold, but they have been enormous.

G. Douglass Lewis
Washington, D.C.
September, 2016

Leadership and Change: A President's Story

Phase I

A Sinking Ship

1982-1985

I. Context and Call

Wesley Seminary moved to Washington, D.C., in 1958. For the next 18 years, it seemed to prosper. Enrollment kept going up, the education program was sound, and the faculty had a distinguished reputation. Because of inflation, however, the school had been spending more than it made. Loans from the endowment fund covered the shortfalls, which appeared too modest to arouse concern. But increasing the deficit while decreasing the endowment fund was like rolling a snowball downhill. In 1977, the hill got dramatically steeper. By 1981, it had become a cliff, and Wesley had reached the brink of extinction—yet nobody seemed aware how grave the situation had become.

In the autumn of 1981, I was one of four candidates for the presidency of Wesley. My wife Shirley and I, and our two children, were then living in Hartford, Connecticut, where I was on the staff of the Hartford Seminary. The chair of Wesley's search committee telephoned in November with the news that I had been selected as the next president.

For 20 years I had felt the desire and the call to become a seminary president. The idea first came to me in the underground stacks of the Duke University library while I was in the Ph.D. program. As I browsed the vast collection during a break, I ran across a book on college and seminary presidents. I was captivated and could not put it down. By the end, I knew what I wanted to be.

We invited some old friends for dinner that evening to celebrate the good news. They teased Shirley and me about adjusting to the new "status" role. Would we even remember our old friends? Could I really deal with the faculty? Could I raise money? What about the church hierarchy and its expectations? Could I still teach? What role would my wife be expected to play?

I laughed and joked with them. We were a close-knit, jubilant group. After they left and we were cleaning up the dishes, Shirley expressed her concern for the first time. She was not sure how she would fit in the role of the president's wife. She was not big on public ceremonies, women's groups, or having to watch what she said to anyone and everyone. She wondered how much entertaining she would be required to do, and if she could continue to work.

Later, after Shirley had gone to bed, I sat by the living room fire with questions of my own. I asked myself if I could I really do the job. My answer was yes, even though I was increasingly aware of how little I knew about being a seminary president. My mother suggested I might be too young, but she was teasing. She had always believed I could accomplish anything, and she had impressed that upon me throughout my formative years. Her efforts were paying dividends for me that evening.

Though I had never had a senior administrative post, I had directed programs, I had taught in a seminary, worked in churches, and participated in quite a number of training programs. In spite of all that, I realized that I did not have a clear vision of what a seminary should be. The search committee had asked me that very question. I had responded with talk about such things as the education of future ministers, relating the seminary more closely to the church, supporting the faculty, generating revenue, balancing the budget, and so forth—a reasonably coherent answer. However, I had stumbled a bit regarding what I thought was the "core mission" of the seminary. Then they asked if I could present a "strategic plan" by the end of year one. I had heard that expression but I had no idea of the specific meaning. I spoke instead about all the planning I had done for various programs and how much I believed in planning, all the while carefully avoiding the word "strategic."

The questions got even harder. What, for example, did I think about distance education, satellite campuses, and non-degree education. I told the committee that I believed the best education took place face-to-face, teacher and student dealing with academic content and spiritual formation together on campus in a community where they could meet in and out of class, worship, and eat together. That response seemed to carry the day. I felt relieved to see most of the committee members nodding their heads as I continued to expound upon what quality education and formation was all about. "That," I said, "is what I am committed to."

Sitting there by the fire as a president-elect in fact and not merely a candidate, I had to admit I was not sure what it would mean to work with the board of governors. I was not sure about the role of the seminary beyond the education of students. I had no inkling of all the issues that would face me when I took office. I was unaware of how changes—within the church and throughout the world—were impacting theological education in North America. I had never had responsibility for dealing day-to-day with the host of issues that seminaries would face as we neared the end of the 20th century. Costs were going up while revenue was declining. Seminary graduates were entering the ministry with ever-increasing debt. Seminaries were about to experience a dramatic change in the makeup of their students. The services that seminaries should provide were changing. Technological developments would challenge every facet of the schools, including libraries, teaching methodologies, and off-campus education. Seminaries, which were opening new programs and new facilities within another school's traditional service area, would introduce a new element of competition. Globalization would become a challenge.

I *did* know that I was committed to the church and its ministry. The church needed effective leaders, and the seminary was the primary educational funnel through which students had to pass on their way into ministerial leadership. I cared about religious institutions and their positive role in the church and the world. I was dedicated to making a seminary the best it could be in that role. I liked people and wanted to help them become the best they could be regardless of their position in an organization. Finally, I believed in myself and my ability to make a positive contribution to whatever group I became a part of. That had been my history.

I was willing to learn what I did not know. I never thought of myself as a savior or a charismatic leader. My style was to function as enabler, an affirmer, and a partner with others in ministry.

On the most important day of my life, I was aware that I had more questions than answers about the job I was assuming. Little did I suspect that I was about to take the helm of a foundering ship.

II. Connecting with the Faculty

In response to the call from the search committee chair, I said I was very honored. However, I could not accept the position without first talking with the Wesley faculty. He was a bit taken aback but agreed that I could come to the campus and meet with them. Two weeks later, Clarence Goen—venerable professor of church history—and his wife Betty took Shirley and me to dinner at De Carlo's in Washington followed by a tour of the campus. I was

5

impressed by his knowledge of Wesley and deeply moved by his love for it.

The next morning we met with the whole faculty, sitting in a circle and fielding their questions. Although not an official interview, it became a moment of tremendous symbolic import. They knew I would not accept the job without talking to them first. They were getting a first-hand, close-up look at the new first family. It was a good opportunity to hear my thoughts with regard to theological education and Wesley's potential. They discovered that I could handle "academic" talk and that I believed a faculty was the core component of a theological school.

The faculty treated me nicely and affirmed me. In the years to come there would be a few times when some of them—occasionally many of them—would have tossed me out gladly. But on that day we had a love-in and committed ourselves to work together toward a grand future for Wesley. None of us knew the gravity of the school's financial situation.

III. The Hidden Crisis

Less than two months after taking office, I received the results of an audit by the CPA firm of Wooden and Benson, summarized in a management letter that said, in part:

> *As shown in the financial statements, the Seminary incurred an excess of expenditures over revenue in the current fund of $369,646 during the year ending June 30, 1982, and, as of that date the total unrestricted liabilities exceeded total assets by $935,003. These factors indicate that the Seminary may be unable to continue in existence.*

I was shocked, and equally surprised to discover the letter also shocked the board of governors. How could such a thing happen without anyone knowing about it? As I probed more deeply, the story began to unfold.

For the first 18 years after Wesley moved to Washington in 1958, it was growing in enrollment, building a good faculty and program, but it did not always achieve an operating surplus. Only in seven of those years did the school have more income than expense in its operating fund. The deficits were not large and were absorbed by increasing a negative fund balance on its fiscal balance sheet, which by 1976 had reached a modest $92,657.

Beginning in fiscal 1976-77, a more dramatic and disastrous decline began. The annual operating budgets showed serious deficits and a growing negative fund balance. In 1976-77, the operating budget was about $1.45 million. By 1981-82 it had increased to $2.5 million.

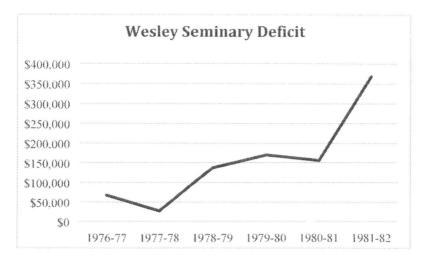

To cover these deficits in its operating budget, the seminary borrowed money from its endowment fund. By

July of 1982 the audited balance sheet showed about $2 million in the endowment, but the seminary had borrowed and spent more than half of that amount. The Board had a policy of paying 8 percent interest on the borrowed amount, but since *no cash repayment was made,* the invested funds just kept on shrinking.

During those years, the board and the president regularly struggled with the financial situation, consistently bemoaning its decline. After reporting on the deficit from the previous year, they would propose a balanced budget for the coming year. They usually did that by projecting more income. That income perennially failed to materialize—thus producing another deficit year. In their oft-stated collective opinion, the problem was inadequate income, not expense growth. They employed a variety of strategies to raise more income, but with little success.

Inflation was rampant during that period, driving up costs and eroding personal spending power. The board, committed to supporting the faculty, tried to keep pace. They voted an 8.5 percent increase in faculty salaries for 1980-81 and 9 percent for 1981-82. Other expenses also grew accordingly.

Depleting the Endowment

The purpose of an endowment is to provide a steady stream of revenue. Adhering to that principle, Wesley apportioned an amount from its invested funds to the operating fund each year. In the early 1970s, the percentage apportioned was not excessive, though it did exceed the 5 percent standard recommended by the Association of Theological Schools (ATS). In the face of increasing operational needs, Wesley's annual percentage of withdrawals grew, thus reducing the amount of endowment invested funds.

8

Although unsustainable, this problem was disguised by the accounting practice of showing a theoretical endowment figure on the balance sheet while ignoring the decline of actual endowment invested funds. As the deficits grew, Wesley nevertheless continued to withdraw an increasing percentage from these invested funds annually.

Fiscal Year	Balance Sheet Endowment	Invested Endowment	Funds Apportioned	% Draw
1976-77	1,552,992	1,131,669	75,639	6.7%
1977-78	1,646,710	1,186,174	77,630	6.5%
1978-79	1,983,925	1,387,668	85,388	6.2%
1979-80	1,978,349	1,171,869	116,440	9.9%
1980-81	2,104,163	1,128,517	156,189	13.8%
1981-82	2,079,297	762,023	177,122	23.2%

In 1981-82 the $177,122 apportioned from the endowment to the operating fund plus the $369,646 borrowed from the endowment to cover the deficit meant that Wesley withdrew $546,768 from its fast-fading endowment in that fiscal year. Only $762,023 of invested funds remained at the end of the 1981-82 fiscal year.

As the auditor's management letter recognized, Wesley Seminary was rapidly going broke.

IV. Having A Gift of Advance Time

I accepted the job in December, 1981, but was not scheduled to take office until July 1, 1982. My then-current position at Hartford Seminary was flexible. The president there allowed me to spend as much time as I needed on Wesley matters.

I have often thought that my six-month head start, functioning as the president unofficially, before Wesley ever paid me a dime, was one of the most important six months of my presidency. Some of the things I was able to initiate, contacts I made, the tone I set, and decisions I made—those were all fundamental to launching my presidency and turning the seminary in a new direction. Few new presidents have such a gift of time and opportunity. For Wesley and for me, it was pivotal.

I did not arrive with a fully-developed vision or plan for the future. Even so, everyone, no matter what their position or relationship to the seminary, wanted to know what the new president thought about Wesley and its future.

It seemed almost daily that I was asked to "say a few words." Sometimes the occasion would call for a formal speech or sermon. Most of the time it was an informal moment—greeting visitors or reporting to the board, faculty, students, church leaders, or lay groups. No matter what the occasion, though, people wanted to hear what the president had to say.

I was surprised—shocked is a better term—to discover that people listened to what I said. That was a new experience. They also *remembered* it, often *quoted it*, even if they put their own spin on it. I realized I needed to be thoughtful, sensitive, even careful about how I spoke and what I said.

On a larger scale without even knowing it, I became an educator, mostly informal. I was, in fact, helping myself and others to grasp the reality of Wesley Seminary and its mission, our worldly context, challenges we faced, and the great opportunities we had to serve and influence that world.

I also learned that many people in the community had their own ideas about what should be happening at Wesley. They often took it upon themselves to "advise" the new president. More than once, I heard suggestions that some individuals employed by the school were inadequate performers at best. They often were identified by name. Of course, some of those who advised me about others would themselves be the objects for recommended exits by the same people they hoped to see depart.

I gradually learned that I was "never not the president"—in the eyes and ears of the Wesley community. At first I did not fully understand this authority conveyed to the president. A misuse or betrayal of this power and influence will inevitably become destructive to the institution and the leader. I subsequently learned not to misuse the trust and influence people granted me and to use it for the benefit of the seminary, never for my personal advantage.

V. Presidential Quarters

When the chair of the presidential search committee called me, he said "a beautiful home" was part of the compensation package. During our first visit to the campus, Shirley and I were anxious to see our new residence on 6 Wesley Circle, but the current president and his wife were out of town, so we could not go inside. Our host then pointed out the "original" presidential quarters on the campus nearby. The house at 6 Wesley Circle, he explained, had been given to the seminary some eight years earlier by a retiring senator. It became the president's home at that time. The original quarters—renamed the Alumni House—had been converted to accommodate the development office on the ground floor. Its three upstairs bedrooms were used for seminary guests. I became one of those guests when I was making regular trips to Washington during the months prior to taking office.

A member of the search committee had told me that Shirley and I were free to choose either of those two houses. We immediately opted for the Alumni House because of its greater potential in terms of entertainment, access to the campus, and suitability to our family's needs. Little did I imagine that decision would become a controversial issue with the board that spring. As I would later discover, some board members held the strong opinion that the president should continue to live at 6 Wesley Circle. Many board members thought it would be very expensive to renovate Alumni House and move the development office into the administration building on campus. Wesley, after all, was in a financial pinch.

I soon realized this conflict could become a disruptive issue even before I took office. (How many undisciplined fights have started over seemingly insignificant debates such as design of a church kitchen!) For Shirley and me, the matter was not insignificant. The original house was clearly more suited to our needs. Even more important, we wanted to change the cultural atmosphere at Wesley. We wanted to send the message that Wesley was a community that must pull together, share together, and—when possible—play together. We wanted a place where we could welcome the community, and that meant playing host to various groups and individuals in comfortable surroundings. We later estimated that during our two decades at Wesley more than 5000 individuals attended events in the president's house.

Shirley grew up in a small town in Tennessee where her family ran the general store. She never regarded herself as being sophisticated. I sometimes teased her about having a "country store" personality. She was friendly and easy-going with people from all walks of life. Despite the affirmation of many, she had trouble believing the Wesley community took delight in her presence and considered her an asset. Over the years, we hosted board members, faculty, staff, students, the Women's Guild, bishops, visiting dignitaries, and quite a few friends and family. Entertaining is not unusual for presidents. Some might say it comes with the job, but we always tried to convey to our guests the feeling they had been invited to our home as well as to a part of the seminary.

Many stories illustrate the hospitality aspect of our ministry at Wesley. One in particular shows the importance and sometimes delicate nature of playing host. During our first Christmas season at Wesley, Shirley and I decided to have a sit-down dinner for the faculty and their spouses. That had never been done before; it was part of our effort to effect change. As we made our preparations we wondered: Should we serve alcohol? Before coming to Wesley, we routinely served wine to dinner guests. But we knew that Methodist tradition was ambiguous when it came to alcoholic beverages. Wine was never served at any seminary function except chapel communion. Even then, grape juice was near at hand. Some Wesley faculty members had strong aversions to serving any alcoholic beverage at any time. So what should we do?

After considerable thought and discussion, we adopted a policy of offering nothing stronger than wine and always having nonalcoholic drinks available. Further, we would pay for wine served at official occasions and never charge it to the entertainment expense account.

The big moment arrived. The house was festive with Christmas decorations as we greeted dozens of faculty members and their spouses. Although a few were obviously perturbed, we heard no comments. The great majority partook of the wine with gusto, laughing and clearly embracing the new policy. As the evening progressed, the venerable professor Clarence Goen told Shirley that she had made history by serving wine for the first time in the president's house. Then he paused, grinned, and said "And I am glad."

Resolving the Conflict

The housing situation dragged on. After discussions in February, the board examined the cost and feasibility of moving the development office into the administration building. In May, after still more discussion, the board, in light of financial uncertainties, decided by split vote that its new president should live at 6 Wesley Circle. In spite of my feelings, I did not think it was the right time to turn that into a do-or-die issue. The decision also left the development office location in limbo.

Some board members who had been involved with the issue from the beginning felt the board had made a bad decision. Wayne Smithey, the newly-elected chair of the board, put together a group to consider different options. They determined that moving the development office could be done at a very low cost. Smithey then called a special meeting of the executive committee to re-consider the previous decision. At his urging, I drafted a memo for the committee in which I first acknowledged the need for fiscal prudence. I then noted that the Development Office would be more efficient in its new location and that the Alumni House was more appropriately designed for presidential functions.

The executive committee then voted to (a) move development to the administration building; (b) make Alumni House the official residence of the president; and (c) rent out 6 Wesley Circle for one year while considering its long-term use or outright sale. The vote was unanimous.

Smithey then called a special meeting of the full board for July 1—my first day in office—to consider those recommendations and to determine new committee assignments for board members. He had the executive committee members contact all board members to share the decision and announce why he was calling a special meeting of the board.

Meanwhile, as some of the board members continued to look at other options, one of them proposed that her family's foundation lend the seminary $30,000 to refurbish the Alumni House. The full board passed all the recommendations unanimously, including acceptance of the foundation loan.

The rush was on to move the Development Office. It took less than a month to do that, and two months to refurbish Alumni House. At the end of August, Shirley and I moved in with our two children just ahead of the fall term. A new era had begun.

VI. New Initiatives

My pre-presidential six months included visiting Wesley on a regular basis for two or three days at a time. Occupying the master bedroom over the development office gave me a first-hand look at the personnel and workings of the development office. The director of development was Bess Jones, who had been at Wesley from its first day on the Washington campus in 1958. She had served as President Trott's secretary, later as

15

director of development and alumni affairs. She was a treasure trove of information about people who had been supporters of Wesley, as well as potential prospects. She was devoted to Wesley and graciously took me under her wing, educating me about the key individuals and donors I should meet. She even went along on many calls to introduce me in those early days.

Bess was also mother hen to the Women's Guild, an organization formed early in the Trott years. The Guild gave money to support the seminary, especially scholarships and special services for the students. I could scarcely believe they actually recruited local churches to bring a meal to campus for students every Saturday evening. They also maintained a clothes closet in the president's house for needy students. The Women's Guild and its associated organization, Epworth House, were high maintenance; they consumed a lot of development office time and energy. Little did I know, back then, that the women who were connected to the seminary through the Guild and Epworth House would give thousands, even millions of dollars to Wesley during the next quarter of a century. Bess made sure that I knew the Guild, its members, its mission, and their desire for presidential attention.

Wesley had launched a Centennial Campaign several years earlier with a goal of raising $2 million dollars. It fell well short of the goal and had been a significant disappointment. The board subsequently abandoned the campaign and shifted development efforts toward the annual fund.

What quickly became evident to me was that Wesley had no up-to-date understanding of fundraising and no effective strategy for generating gift income. The seminary had not succeeded in building its donor base to keep pace with increased costs. Very early I concluded that we had to start fresh, by moving the development offices out of the house to the administration building, recruit new leadership, invest presidential energy in fundraising, and lift our sights higher.

By the end of February I shared my judgment with members of the small committee set up by the board to work with me on the transition. I also told them that I knew some things about fundraising and was dedicated to working on it myself. However, I thought we needed a development consultant to help us start from scratch, building from the ground up a new fundraising program for the seminary. They agreed with my judgments and recommendations and served as an informal search committee in the hunt for a consultant. We interviewed four candidates and selected Tom Broce, whom I had known at Duke many years before. Broce had been a young director of development at Duke, the vice president for development at Southern Methodist, and then president of Phillips University. He had moved to full-time fundraising consulting a few years before.

I remember the big lump in my throat when he told me his fee schedule—$2,400 a month for 10 months, plus expenses. He would be on the Wesley campus two days a month and available anytime by phone. "Wow," I thought, "that is proportionally more than Wesley is paying its president." The board committee agreed to the contract and confirmed the decision with the executive committee of the board. Tom began working with me immediately, and it proved to be the best investment we could have made.

Finding New Personnel

We got an extra bonus that spring without having to look for it. A first-year Wesley student named David Wilson was working in the development office and he seemed to know what went on there—as well as what did not. He was a bright, energetic young man who wanted to take part in the conversations when Tom and I had our heads together. Over the years I teased David by saying that we couldn't get rid of him in those days. The truth was that he was enormously helpful and would become increasingly important to us as time went on. He became an essential cog in the new development effort and ultimately succeeded me as president of Wesley Seminary. Neither he nor I could have imagined that would come to pass.

Meanwhile, Tom and I already had started a search for vice president for development. I wanted someone committed to theological education, who knew the church, was goal-driven and willing to take on the daunting task of raising large sums of money for a seminary during hard times. We advertised locally and sought recommendations but found no one who seemed to fit the bill.

A member of the presidential search committee suggested that I talk with Lovett Weems, who was a DMin graduate from Wesley, currently serving as a pastor in Mississippi. Lovett had an excellent reputation as a minister, organizer, and hard worker. I was delighted when he agreed to talk with us.

Tom and I spent a full afternoon with Lovett in July and came away disillusioned. We had done most of the talking; our candidate had said almost nothing. He asked a few questions and listened to us talk about development. Tom invited him to dinner that evening. When we met again the next morning, I was wondering what we would talk about for three hours. To our surprise and delight, Lovett began laying out what he saw as the major tasks in development at Wesley and how he would tackle them. He described how he would approach the job and what help he would need. The excitement that he demonstrated about the job and his enthusiasm for Wesley had been completely missing the previous afternoon. By the end of the morning, I was so pleased that I not only offered him the job, I felt like giving him a big hug. He said yes, with the stipulation that he would first like to talk with his wife, his bishop, and leaders within his congregation.

Little did I realize that morning that we had just put together the "development formidable foursome"— Lewis, Broce, Weems, and Wilson—who over the next three years would elevate the development program to new heights and lay the groundwork for an extraordinary climb to financial sustainability and prosperity. Over the next 20 years we would move Wesley to an annual fund of a million dollars and conduct three successful capital campaigns that would produce almost $70 million.

From the perspective of that day in July of 1982, our future accomplishments would have appeared as pure fantasy. We had only dedication and enthusiasm going for us at that moment. The hard work of putting a plan together and executing it lay ahead. That process would involve too many details to enumerate. The guiding principles, however—the building blocks—may be useful to others faced with a task so difficult that it seems impossible.

Building the Development Program

Presidential commitment and involvement in fundraising, I soon recognized, would be critical if we were to succeed. I had never done much direct fundraising, but I was committed to doing it because we needed it.

Some personal characteristics are helpful in fundraising. There is no substitute for liking people and enjoying relationships you build with them. Listening and learning what is important to potential donors gives insight to their motivation. Keeping the institution's needs in mind is equally important. Those two factors are the primary ingredients of a successful relationship. They must always be kept in mind and always kept in balance.

Over the years, people would ask me if I ever got tired of fundraising. My answer became standard: No! It is actually fun and the most meaningful thing I do. Fellow seminary presidents would ask how often I thought about fundraising. My answer: Every day.

Those who invested in Wesley flowed in and out of my life, my consciousness, and my prayers. I was always thinking about how to be in touch. What were they thinking? What was important to them? When was it appropriate for me to ask them for a gift to Wesley? Even now, 30 years later, I still cherish the memory of Wesley supporters. In giving to the seminary they were giving me their trust, and that has enriched my life beyond measure.

An Excellent Staff was the second building block in fundraising. Wesley and its grateful president were extremely fortunate when Lovett Weems agreed to become vice president for development. Like me, he had a limited background in fundraising, but he had the drive and dedication to succeed. He lived and breathed Wesley and was consumed with thoughts of how to raise money to support its ministry. He was goal-driven, exceptionally well-organized, and a workaholic of the first order.

Although just a young student, David Wilson (McAllister-Wilson after he married a year later) had the drive, the interest, and the commitment that made him a key player on the team. We quickly recognized his unique combination of talents and loaded him up with work, which he loved. He and Lovett became an inseparable pair, totally committed to the success of the program. They even worked together in the mountains of Colorado while David was there on his honeymoon.

Regular contact with consultant. Two days a month with Tom Broce turned out to be our third component of success. Lovett, David, and I wondered, early on, if we could spare that much time away from our busy schedules. We got antsy thinking of other things we needed to be doing. Years would go by before I came to realize the importance of those two days with Tom every month.

That time away from our everyday duties forced us to concentrate purely on development. It became an accountability session for us to report on what we were doing, for better or worse. That would set the stage for us to plan our next steps. Tom would remind us that a lot of shoe leather was necessary in fundraising. That was his not-so-subtle way of telling us to get out of the office, meet people, and talk about the seminary.

"Ask for their support," he would say. Anyone who has done fundraising and is honest about it will tell you how easy it is to fill your daily schedule with stuff that produces very few dollars coming in the door. In a gentle, often humorous way, Tom pushed us to set concrete goals, pursue them, and report to each other on the outcome. Eventually we became knowledgeable, downright expert, in fundraising theory and practice. We had to do it, though, and not just talk about it. Our development office had to be organized so as to track prospects, record gifts, organize events, outline goals to be reached, and so on and so on. Without realizing it, we were absorbing the fourth component: **learn the basics.**

Those two-day confabulations were a combination of hard work, fun, and productivity. They facilitated a bonding process; we developed an *esprit de corps* which served us well through good times and hard times for more than 30 years.

As a former college president, Tom's understanding of the challenges facing me went beyond fundraising. We discussed a wide range of issues that confront every president. That was an added benefit of his time with us, something most presidents never experience. Over the years I have encouraged countless numbers of seminary presidents to find themselves a listening ear—a strategic partner, if you will.

Tom stayed in our home during his monthly visits for a span of five years. He became a part of our family fellowship. That was far longer that it took for us to learn all he knew about fundraising, but he was an integral cog in our machinery during those demanding years of change. We were lucky to have him.

During one of Tom's visits in May of 1986, Shirley created a spectacular meal of duck *à l'orange*. Tom was on cloud nine. He loved being in our home and he loved Shirley's cooking. That evening was like a celebration for all we had been through together. He flew home to Dallas the next day, which was a Friday. He went out for a run the next morning and dropped dead from a heart attack. He was 54. It was a stunning blow to his family and friends—especially to Wesley Seminary and the young president who owed so much to a very special friend and mentor.

VII. Fundraising

At the beginning of my plunge into fundraising I had little knowledge of its theory and practice. Gradually four basic steps of fundraising emerged from a lot of on-the-job experience: **Identify, Cultivate, Ask, and Thank**. All our efforts revolved around those steps. They were easy to memorize, but it took persistence and focus to make them effective.

Who potentially cared enough about Wesley and its mission to give money to support it? Personally, I considered everybody a prospect. That did not always prove to be the case, of course. But a constituency of supporters is the foundation of a sustainable institution, and for us to build a strong constituency, we had to reach out in all directions. We constantly looked for individuals, groups, and organizations with whom to share the Wesley story and invited them to become a part of our extended community.

Tom proposed a new idea: forming a "Wesley Council" made up of people who give $1000 or more every year. We all gasped. I did not know anybody I thought could or would give a $1000 to Wesley Seminary. Tom persisted. He insisted that there were people who could and would write checks of that size to support the seminary. We just had to find them and ask them.

I pointed out that a survey of our seminary's previous contributions showed only a small number of gifts that large. Tom then said the president himself—me—should be the first one to write a check for $1000. I had never given that much to any charity in my life, much less asked anybody else to do it. While I was trying to get over the

23

shock, Tom went on to say that once I had made that donation, I should ask the chair of the board to do the same thing.

I took that advice, made the first gift, approached the chair, and—sure enough—he matched my contribution.

Several board members volunteered to host a "dessert" and invite people they knew who might be good prospects for the Wesley Council. At one of these early gatherings, hosted by Helen Wicklein, a member of the board of governors from Baltimore, I committed one of my famous gaffes. After dessert, I began my remarks about Wesley and its mission and our need to broaden the base of involvement and investment inside and outside the institution.

Always searching for new imagery, I said, "We have two important groups at the seminary. One is the on-campus folk who are engaged daily in educational work. The other is those folk out in communities and churches like yours who are an extension of Wesley and who provide support that allows the educational work to go on. We call those on campus the 'In-House' group. Then there are those, like yourselves, whom we call the 'Out-House' group."

A moment of silence ensued, followed by a rousing burst of laughter kicked off by my esteemed colleagues, Mr. Weems and Mr. Wilson.

The Outhouse speech took its place in the annals of our development lore. I was reminded of it countless times  throughout my presidency. It became, in fact, one of my best entrées into talking about the inside and outside realities of the Wesley constituency. When I retired twenty years later, Randal Adams from the building and grounds staff made and presented me with a small handcrafted wooden model of an outhouse with DOUG graphically displayed above the door.

To our great surprise and delight, many people began to step up, write a $1000 check, expand the Wesley Council, and make it a critical component of the Wesley turnaround. I could hardly believe how many people came out of the woodwork to join this new venture. One Saturday morning, an older gentleman named Print Hudson appeared at my doorstep. I had gotten to know him at one of our events and remembered him well because of our shared West Tennessee roots. He said, "Doug, you know that Council you have been talking about? Well, my wife Grace and I like the idea and want to join. I will be sending you a $1,000 check today."

Having said his piece, he turned and left. Print was a man of few words. I was almost in tears and my heart was nearly bursting with joy and gratitude.

Like so many, Print's gift was more than money; it was an affirmation of Wesley, the importance of its mission, and of me personally. I served merely as the conduit for people to invest in something that touched their deepest hopes and dreams. Who would not want the privilege of witnessing those miracles firsthand?

Prospects came forth in many ways. We learned to stay alert to new prospects and respond to them faithfully and caringly. Dr. Margaret Pittman, the first female scientist at the National Institutes of Health, was among the guests at a special dinner following my inauguration in the fall of 1982. She turned to faculty member Jim Clemons and said, "When is Wesley going help my church that is struggling and losing members?"

When Jim later shared that conversation with us, David Wilson called upon Dr. Pittman. Her church, Mount Vernon Place United Methodist, was located in downtown Washington. Its membership had gradually declined from 4,500 to less than 150. Dr. Pittman had a passion for urban ministry and wanted Wesley to prepare its students to serve in urban areas and resuscitate churches like hers. Upon meeting David, she immediately recruited him to teach her Sunday School class. It was called the All States class because at one time it had a member from every state in the Union. Periodically for the next few years, David taught that class and the John Rustin class—both made up of older, long-standing members of Mt. Vernon Place. Through David and Dr. Pittman's involvement at Wesley, she became a major donor and built an endowment for Wesley's urban ministry program.

Several other donors emerged from those classes. From that unprepossessing initial encounter with Dr. Pittman, thanks to David's continuing engagement, Wesley eventually received almost $4 million.

Mount Vernon Place sold its large but lightly-used educational building in 2003. David was the catalyst behind that venture. By then president of Wesley, he organized a partnership consisting of Mount Vernon Place, Wesley, and the Baltimore-Washington Annual

Conference of the United Methodist Church. The old building was replaced by a new high-rise with the first three floors dedicated to church and faculty offices, 18 dormitory rooms, and educational space for Wesley's urban ministry and public policy programs. Dr. Pittman had passed on, but there can be no doubt she would have been excited and proud.

We also spoke with many other church groups about the seminary and its mission, inviting them to become a part of the extended Wesley community. Many congregations became Wesley Council members. Ten years later, those early contacts opened the door to a significant identity change for Wesley. They led the way in establishing an interactive network of partner congregations as Wesley began to fulfill its mission as a church-based theological school.

We were reminded daily that fundraising was about relationships built on trust, affirmation, and a desire to invest in something important. I believe every human being has deeply-held values and desires. Finding the place and the means of investing in them is the challenge. Seminary development means connecting the human desire to give and make a difference with the mission of a seminary as a vehicle for that investment.

Cultivating Prospects and Donors

Building a list of donor prospects required finding candidates with both interest and resources. Many people think fundraising is simply identifying a few very rich people and asking them to give. Almost from my first day at Wesley, people would advise me to go see Frank Perdue. He had made millions in the chicken-processing business. He attended a United Methodist Church on the Eastern Shore of Maryland, which has the highest percentage of Methodists of any area in America. More than three-fourths of all the United Methodist pastors in that area were graduates of Wesley.

I did meet Frank Perdue and subsequently visited him and his wife several times. I reminded him that all the pastors of his church were Wesley grads, and I asked him for financial support for the seminary. While gracious, he was emphatic in being averse to sending money away from the Eastern Shore—especially to Washington. We had enjoyable conversations, but the financial results came to exactly nothing. That was a significant lesson for me: a donor with money must also have the motivation. It also drove home the lesson that Wesley could not speed up its progress by merely soliciting major gifts from a few wealthy people.

The Frank Perdue case reminded me of the old saying: there is more than one way to skin a cat. He finally did support Wesley, although not in the manner or the timeframe I had envisioned. A good friend of mine from the Eastern Shore advised me: "Doug, I grew up on the Eastern Shore. You have to understand that folk here are very careful with their money. They want to keep it close to home, always. You have to devise a means by which they can invest in the seminary and the Eastern Shore at the same time."

With his encouragement, we set up the Eastern Shore Pastoral Scholarship Fund through a local community foundation. Those who gave money to that fund could be sure that it went for scholarships to Eastern Shore students preparing for ministry—at Wesley Seminary.

A few years later, the Kresge Foundation made a $4 million challenge grant to the community foundation. Frank Perdue then added $1 million to encourage other groups. He and the Kresge grant would match the amount each group would raise. Wesley applied for a $100,000 challenge, received it, and subsequently raised the $100,000. It was matched by none other than Frank Perdue. My original "ask" had a very long tail and it ended up larger than either of us had imagined. That fund continues to grow and provide scholarships for Wesley students from the Eastern Shore.

In our early days we also identified two other wealthy prospects. As a staff, we often told each other that we could not meet our fundraising goals without a major gift from each of them. The fact is, we never received a major gift from either one—ever. Even when they went to their graves, they left us nothing. One of them became a good friend. I probably visited with him a couple of dozen times, the last occasion being his funeral.

We learned that fundraising is a long-term proposition. It begins with a core group of individuals who believe in the seminary and invest in it. New prospects usually come one at a time. One of them connects you with the next one, and so on and on. Sometimes it felt excruciatingly slow, even hopeless, to attain the lofty goals we had set. The process never ends, even after the person becomes a regular donor. Sometimes it seemed that we perhaps should spend more time with our current donors than with prospects. We learned, however, that it's not a matter of one or the other—it's both.

Late in our first year we began a "special event" strategy that combined the affirmation of current donors and the cultivation of new ones at the same time. We invited Wesley Council members for lunch on campus, along with members of the board and new prospects. Lunch would be followed by some Washington event such as a visit to the Supreme Court, the National Gallery of Art, or the newly-renovated Union Station. Some Wesley faculty members even wanted to join the group. Those get-togethers helped us form a community of people who shared a common interest in the mission of the seminary.

Three Types of Gifts

The most effective and successful development programs are those which continually work on three types of gifts, regularly and persistently. The first was an *annual gift* that helped us meet our annual fund goals but also kept the individual connected to Wesley on a continuing basis.

Second, we wanted *a large gift for a designated purpose*, usually generated by means of a capital campaign. Most donors who have been giving to a school for several years will at some point make a special-purpose contribution 10 times larger than their annual gift. A contribution such as that would be rare from someone who has never previously given to the institution. (The exception would be a foundation or other agency with an interest in some special cause.)

Wesley had conducted only one capital campaign in its history, and it had not been successful. In our new development program, we plugged away almost four years building a donor base before launching a capital campaign—and it worked better than expected.

The third type of contribution we looked for was inclusion in *the estate plan* of each donor. Individuals almost always have more money to give in their estate than they do for annual or capital gifts. Putting the seminary in one's will usually occurs only when a person has had a long-term relationship with the school. One problem is that most people are not very good planners in the matter of their estate. It requires special persistence, nurturing, and—often—assistance to help the donor make that decision and follow through on it. We worked with one person for almost two years before he figured out exactly how he could and would include Wesley in his estate plan.

Asking for a Gift

Tom Broce reminded us that Wesley would receive very few checks that we had not asked for. He was right. Identifying and cultivating prospects was not enough. We had to provide the opportunity for someone to consider making a gift. Our wise and wily bishop, Fred Wertz, a member of the Wesley board who had been a college president, advised us, "You do not have to protect donors; they will do that for themselves. You must make sure they have the opportunity to consider a gift decision that only they can make."

At first I wondered if I could consistently and persistently ask people for money. During the next few years I came to understand that people *expected* me to ask. I also learned that the more specific I could be about an amount and a purpose for the gift, the more helpful it was to an individual donor. The "ask" gave them something concrete to consider, a choice to make, and a vision of how they could contribute to something significant and meaningful. It not only helped Wesley, it rewarded them as well. Their decisions disappointed me many times, but I tried never to let that influence how I related to them. On the other hand, I did not allow a "no" to discourage me.

I soon recognized that most of us church-folk are ambivalent about money, both the askers and the givers. Almost everybody is a bit suspicious of those who openly talk about money. One of my favorite Wesley supporters was an older woman of some financial means. I always enjoyed my visits and conversations with her. I loved her stories and especially her candid, forceful manner. I regularly thanked her for her support and invited her to continue it. On one occasion she told me that her friends claimed I only came to see her to get her money. I asked her how she responded to them. In a flash, she said she told them she didn't care—she liked me anyway.

I came to believe that deep down, all humans have a desire to do something significant with their lives. We spend most of our days searching for what we can best invest ourselves in and find ways to do that. My vocation was to listen deeply to people and explore with them ways to invest. One consideration I always presented was Wesley Seminary as being vital to the church, the culture, and to them. It was up to them to decide whether that should be one of the means by which they could achieve personal fulfillment.

Thanking Donors

Nothing in development work is more important than thanking the donor. When and how to do that may vary, but it is critical. Most people who make charitable gifts rarely receive a timely thank-you. Tom said thanks should go out the very next day after receipt of the gift.

We were less than perfect in our follow-up, but we always stressed remembering each donor and each gift. I made it a practice to acknowledge each gift of $100 or more with a signed note. I also wrote a personal a letter to acknowledge every Wesley Council gift.

Shirley had been a teacher throughout our marriage. She supported me through seminary and graduate school. After we moved to Wesley, she decided that selling real estate would be an interesting challenge that would also help her learn the city of Washington. She was right, and it also enriched our lives with a stream of good stories.

One of her first commissions came to $950, which she decided to donate to Wesley. Shortly thereafter, she received a letter from Lovett Weems saying, "Shirley, if you would add an additional $50 to your gift, you would become a member of the Wesley Council and you would receive a personal letter from the president." She added the $50, and I wrote the letter. I wish I had a copy of it.

I do not know how many personal thank-you cards and letters I wrote during my 20 years at Wesley. What I do know is that each one, even in a small way, contributed to the bond between the members of our growing support constituency and the seminary. I always insisted on signing two things: donor letters and diplomas.

Publishing the names of contributors was a more debatable form of acknowledgement. Although Wesley had not been doing that, we did so only after careful consideration. Tom pushed us to start doing it. He said people want their gifts to be recognized. At first, we merely published a list of all donors regardless of amount. We then decided to list Wesley Council members separately, and ultimately to develop categories according to the size of the gift and publish the names under each category.

It could be argued that Christians should not seek public recognition for their gifts. On the other hand, all of us had to confess we wanted our names on the list and that we carefully scanned it to see who else was on it and how much they gave. We had very few donors who insisted their gifts be anonymous. The most positive spin I finally could put on the matter is that public recognition of a person's gift served as a model to encourage others to follow suit. It provided testimony that such-and-such person believed in and supported the mission of Wesley

Seminary. The categories became goals toward which others could strive.

We also discovered that our success rate was improved by assigning current donors to the "asking" teams.

A Nice Surprise

One Saturday morning in the middle of June, 1983, I received a phone call from Helen Smith, an active and dedicated board member. She and her husband Gordon were sitting at the breakfast table talking about the tremendous progress Wesley had made in the last year. They wanted to know how close we were to balancing the budget for that year. I did not have the actual numbers at hand, but I told her it appeared that we were within $50 thousand of that goal. Helen then said that she and Gordon were wondering if a check for $15 thousand would help. One can easily imagine my response.

The following Monday morning found our team working feverishly on a letter to our donor list recounting how we had just received a generous gift that brought us within striking range of a balanced budget. We challenged our friends to make additional gifts that might put us over the top. Within two weeks the challenge brought in $35,125. We balanced the budget.

Year-End Results

Our fundraising results for the first year—1982-83—far exceeded expectations. The seminary had raised only $309,000 the previous year. We topped out at $465,000. In gifts for all purposes, we did even better by raising almost $602,000 compared to a previous total of not quite $366,000.

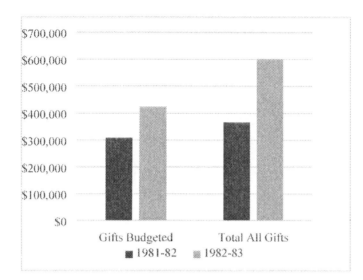

When the auditors presented their 1982-83 fiscal year report, it showed a positive balance of $54,361 versus a deficit of $369,366 for the previous year.

Oddly enough, we had not concentrated on dollar-amount goals; we had focused on the number of new Wesley Council gifts we could generate.

VIII. Developing the Board of Governors

Wesley's bylaws contained some interesting requirements for the board of governors. The board would consist of four classes, each class serving four-year terms, with a maximum of three consecutive terms. Each class would have 6 to 10 members, which meant there would be at least 24 members and not more than 40. All of them had to be members of the United Methodist Church, and half of them had to be clergy. Each class was required to have at least two Wesley alumni, two women, and two black individuals (the term used in the bylaws). The original motivation was laudable, designed to represent the diversity and social commitments of the United Methodist Church and to affirm the seminary's roots in that denomination.

Although not a bylaw requirement, an informal tradition also shaped the selection of officers of the board. The position of chair rotated between a clergy and a layperson, with no specified length of term. The usual succession moved the vice-chair to chair. There was a geographical spread over the annual conferences of the Northeast Jurisdiction of the UMC. The dominant part of the membership came from the Baltimore and Washington areas. The Virginia annual conference, however, was only sparsely represented in spite of being the largest in the UMC.

Ideally, board members should be qualified to govern—to make hard decisions, to understand financial management, and to make significant financial contributions. The bylaws, however, were designed to produce a representative board. As a result, the selection process tended more toward filling slots to meet the bylaw requirements than selection of highly-qualified members. We ended up with a membership characterized by earnest people with good intentions—which almost paved the road to Wesley's demise. Close to a third of its members made no annual gifts. Several of the board meetings failed to produce a quorum necessary to take official action.

I had been around educational institutions long enough to know that a strong seminary required a strong board. I also knew that boards could not be transformed quickly. It was apparent to me that I was facing an uphill climb that could last 10 years or more. It would progress one plodding step at a time, and it had to begin right away.

<u>Selecting a New Board Chair</u>

During one of my visits to the campus in April of 1982, I met with the board's nominating committee. It was about to propose a slate of officers for the coming year. The full board would vote on those recommendations in May. Only three members of that committee showed up, and they considered their task to be simple enough. The chair of the board, a clergy member from Baltimore, was retiring. All three committee members quickly agreed to follow tradition and advance the vice-chair, a layperson, into the lead position. I felt uncomfortable about that move and offered an observation. I reminded them that Wesley had just completed a year-long, national search for a new president. The next most important leadership role in the seminary was the chair of the board of governors. I suggested that in light of that critical moment in Wesley's history, the committee might want to interview several board members who seemed to have potential as a board chair before making its final recommendation for such a vital position.

Their response was immediate and enthusiastic. They devoted the rest of the meeting to reviewing the list of board members and deciding whom they would interview. Together, we designed an interview process that included a set of pertinent questions. During the next three weeks they interviewed several candidates before selecting Wayne Smithey by unanimous vote.

At the May meeting of the full board, all of the committee's recommended officers were elected unanimously and enthusiastically—initial surprise notwithstanding.

Wayne Smithey, who was vice president of Ford Motor Company in Washington, became an outstanding leader of the Wesley board during his four-year term. He was the perfect choice for a new president just then developing his sea legs. He and I talked frequently. He always had a series of pointed questions about whatever issues were before us. He made sure I considered the issues from all sides, developed my position, and was prepared to defend it. After grilling me thoroughly, he would support me 100 percent. Wayne also knew how to manage meetings efficiently and effectively. The first building block of a strong board had been cemented into place.

Changing the Bylaws

The second suggestion I made to the nominating committee that day in April of 1982 was to consider reviewing the bylaws to identify possible changes in the makeup of the board and the criteria by which members were chosen. Again, they were enthusiastic about that idea. The implementation took longer and required much more thought and effort—almost a year, in fact. But the changes were dramatic and resulted in the establishment a new kind of membership. Repopulating the board took almost another 10 years, but it opened new doors of support, revealed new visions about the board's mission, and gave us a governing body with the creative spark to think and act on the strategic level.

The first change involved characteristics of the membership. They began to recognize that although Wesley was a United Methodist seminary, it attracted a diverse and ecumenical student body and faculty. It needed a board aligned with that reality. The newly-revised bylaws called for only 80 percent of the membership to be United Methodists instead of 100 percent. Some years later, that was further reduced to 66 percent. Membership would continue to be diverse with respect to race, gender, and education level, but no quotas would be specified. Though it was not written into the new bylaws, the board eventually adopted a membership goal of two-thirds lay and one-third clergy. A second building block was now in place.

A Board Development Committee

The next step changed "Nominating Committee" to "Board Development Committee," with a mandate to shape, educate, and evaluate the board members—as opposed to the former practice of merely nominating new members and letting them drift along without guidance. At the end of the development committee's first year, Helen Smith became its chair. She arranged a day-long retreat (a first for the Wesley board) that was held the day before the board meeting in May of 1983. Although not well attended, it did raise the sights of the board with regard to its function and the need to develop its governing capacity.

Helen insisted on a picture directory of members to help them to know each other better and to promote contact between meetings. To provide more informal community building among board members, Shirley and I hosted a dinner after one of the meetings during our first year. Many of the spouses of board members were there. Everyone left with a positive feeling. In my case, that feeling led to an embarrassment.

I was so excited about the spirit generated at that first dinner that I assumed we would make it a new tradition. When the next meeting time rolled around, Shirley went all out with hospitality arrangements highlighted by a fancy dinner. Only one thing was missing: the guests. I had failed to invite anybody.

I had assumed the tradition was in place, but nobody else did. During the afternoon session of the meeting, I casually mentioned something about the dinner. There was a long, deadly silence. Only then did I realize that most of the members had not planned to stay. The old biblical passage urging the host to go out and invite people off the street into the feast suddenly became relevant. A few board members graciously came to dinner, along with what few staff and faculty members I managed to corral. All told, we had about half the number Shirley had prepared for. As she and I were clearing dishes afterward, she said that would be the last board dinner she was going to fix.

It wasn't, though. We had many more board events and dinners in our home over the next 20 years. They were all well-attended and created special memories for everyone. They did become tradition, part of which was that each and every member received a special invitation to each and every event. (As previously mentioned, I was willing to learn.)

A Lilly Grant

I discovered that Lilly Endowment had instituted a new grants program to encourage seminary board development. They were offering a workshop on governance and a small $3,000 grant to each participating seminary. We applied and received our first Lilly grant. Wayne Smithey, Helen Smith, and I attended the day-long workshop. The assignment for participating seminaries was to design a board development plan. Those who presented an acceptable plan and reported on its results a year later would receive a second grant of $3,000. Thus began a long and growing partnership with Lilly Endowment, which would support many innovations at Wesley in the years to come.

The President's Advisory Council

During my first year I discovered that my predecessor had an advisory council that met once a year to talk about what was happening at Wesley and gather suggestions about the seminary's program. The two dozen or so members were half clergy and half laity. I thought that was a good idea, and continued with the group in my first year. The discussion was interesting, but they were mainly asking what I planned for Wesley's future.

During the meeting, one of the lay members took me aside to offer some advice. He believed that clergy and laity should not be together because, as he claimed, the clergy dominated the conversations and showed little interest in the laity's perspective. His suggestion made sense. The seminary environment gave us ample opportunity to explore matters from the clergy point of view. What I needed was a group of lay people to speak about issues concerning them. I needed to understand their feelings about the preparation of their pastors, how well they as church members understood theological schools, and how Wesley could connect better with congregations.

A few weeks after the meeting, I let the group know that I was changing the advisory council to an all-laity group and that we were designing other means to get input from clergy. I invited the lay members of the original council to remain, and I began recruiting others. In doing so, I had the good fortune to meet Arthur Flemming, a distinguished layman who was a dedicated and active United Methodist. Arthur had been a college president, an advisor to several U. S. presidents, and was the first secretary of the Department of Health, Education, and Welfare. He was retired and living in Washington, but still very active in numerous causes. I asked him to consider chairing this new lay advisory group. He immediately accepted, with enthusiasm.

Arthur was a perfect chair. His reputation attracted others, and his style was open and affirming. He wanted everyone to participate in the discussions. He also wanted the group to be helpful to me. He could not abide whiners, complainers, or anyone pushing a personal agenda. In his gentle way he would always steer the conversation back to the matters I wanted us to address.

I did not at first realize what a gift Arthur Flemming was to me at that stage of my life. I had never before had a group of people dedicated to offering me guidance. After several years as chair, Arthur stepped down, he said, to give others an opportunity, but he remained my great supporter and advisor for 10 years. At least twice a year, he would invite me for breakfast or lunch at the Hay Adams Hotel near the White House. We would talk. I would update him on seminary matters, reap some of his wisdom, and return to the campus feeling refreshed and affirmed. I wished that every seminary president could have an Arthur Flemming.

That all-laity advisory council proved to be one of the most helpful elements of my presidency. We began with meetings once a year and soon made it twice a year. Later we invited a lay representative from each of the Wesley Seminary Partner Parishes. I loved it. Whenever I met someone who expressed interest in Wesley and had creative ideas or connections, I could immediately invite that person to become a member of the council. There was no waiting list, no screening committee—just like-minded people desirous of working together on Wesley's issues.

Eventually the council had a membership of 45, and about 30-35 of them showed up regularly. One came from Richmond, another from Wilmington. I designed the meetings around the major challenges we were facing at Wesley at the moment. The group divided into small groups to analyze the issue and propose alternative solutions. Most of the time they would come up with things I had never considered. At various times I would share with them my thoughts and questions: where was theological education in America heading? What is the future of denominations? How shall we fund theological schools? Who was showing up in the student body? How can Wesley relate more directly with local parishes? After every meeting, I would go home full of new ideas, feeling excited and affirmed, proud that the seminary had a group of laity who cared deeply about Wesley.

Several unplanned benefits emerged from the group:

- The members provided a link to their congregations. All agreed to share thoughts about Wesley in their churches. A couple of them even created an informal Wesley newsletter for their church.
- The Council became a "farm system" for the board of governors, as several of them eventually joined the board. Already up to speed on Wesley matters, they hit the ground running.
- We invited all board members to prayerfully consider becoming a member of the Wesley Council; almost half of them did. They also identified other prospects for the Council, including financial support from their churches.
- They all became members of the "Presidential Fan Club." It was a mutual admiration society.

I wish that every seminary president could have a lay advisory council to go along with their Arthur Flemming.

Early Glimpses of Emerging Change

Turning around an educational institution does not take place quickly. It is a long-term undertaking that requires persistent effort and commitment. In the early stages, things moved slower than I wanted. I learned to pay attention to small indications of change. By the end of the first year, glimmers of hope began to appear. We had a topnotch board chair, a board development committee with a new chair, a revised set of bylaws, and a 100 percent increase in the amount of gifts from members of the board.

I worked with the new development committee during the 1982-83 year to find new members who would begin to alter the makeup of the board and expand its representation. By May of 1983, membership included clergy members from the Baltimore, Virginia, Eastern Pennsylvania, Central Pennsylvania, and West Virginia conferences. We also had a strong trio of lay members: Barbara Kettler and Isham Baker from Washington, and Norris Tingle, a lawyer from Baltimore. Barbara would become a key leader and donor in our first capital campaign three years later. Isham, an African-American architect, would chair our first affirmative action committee and later serve as board chair. He became one of the most beloved and admired members of the board.

Evaluating the President

A governing board is responsible for the selection, support, and evaluation of its president—and if necessary, his or her removal. The president serves as the board's agent to lead the institution within the framework and policies set by the board. Unfortunately, many boards underperform in those areas and thus allow the school to drift into detrimental habits. Wayne Smithey was determined to see that did not happen at

44

Wesley. He set up procedures by which he and the board's executive committee would evaluate the president every year, which in the summer of 1983 made me the first one.

I was pleased with the results. The board affirmed my accomplishments while endorsing my plans. That was also an appropriate time to look back on my first year as president. I liked the job. I felt confirmed in my call. Though I had more growth ahead, I felt confident in my ability to do the job well.

Those reflections stirred memories of an informal contract I had with the school. Before I accepted the job, a salary had been mentioned, but nothing was put in writing. During one of my trips to campus in 1981, Doug Cooney took me out to dinner. He was a plain-speaking, up-front member of the board's search committee. He said, "The chair of the board is sick and the chair of the search committee is out of town. Since I am a member of the search committee, they asked me to work out this contract business with you. So tell me what you want and we will work it out."

Somewhat surprised, I told him the aforementioned salary suited me. I did suggest the seminary furnish me a car since I would be traveling quite a bit. I also wanted a small transition fund for the next six months to enable me to visit Wesley regularly and perhaps visit a couple of other schools to learn what they were doing.

He said that was fine. The executive committee later agreed. Although I never received a formal contact, that was not unusual. Across the United States, seminaries did not follow a standard practice in that regard. Some of them had elaborate contracts that spelled out the duties and performance expectations of the president, along with specifics about salary, benefits, housing, and the like. Other schools had a simple letter with start-date and salary—period. My case clearly fit the latter category. Once Doug Cooney said "fine," that was it. From then on, I served "at the pleasure of the board."

That informal agreement never bothered me. If the board cannot get along with the president, he/she simply has to go. The reason does not matter, because the institution will suffer significantly in the face of such conflict. Situations like that do exist and go unresolved in many seminaries, usually producing grievous results.

IX. Building the Senior Management Team

The senior leadership team, like the board, would have a strong influence on our chance for success. Jim Collins' famous leadership metaphor—getting the right people on the bus and in the right seats—would not be published for another two decades, but I knew the truth of that principle from day one. What I could not have articulated precisely were the criteria by which a leader should select the right people. How does one go about doing that?

I regarded myself as open and supportive of others. I was more interested in accomplishments for Wesley than who got the credit. My goal was to recruit others to become better than they had imagined. That called for decisions more consequential than any others in my life except the time I asked Shirley Savage to be my wife. That turned out quite well, though, so I pronounced myself qualified to keep on making bold decisions.

The Wesley bus was already loaded. I stepped aboard wondering who should stay, who should go, and what would be the price of change.

Business Manager

I soon had a growing concern about the business office. The auditors had uncovered irregularities and some funds unaccounted for. Subsequent investigation led to the dismissal of a couple of staff. Our business manager was good in the accounting area but was overloaded trying to supervise other operational areas, such as building and grounds, food service, and bookstore. Near the end of my first year, after consultations with the finance committee of the board, I asked him to serve as comptroller and oversee the regular accounting tasks. I persuaded Doug Cooney to become the business manager reporting to me, serving as a member of the administrative council, and having general oversight of the business office and all internal management areas.

Doug had been the pastor of a large church, a district superintendent, and a member of the Wesley board. He had great people skills, a practical bent, and a "take-charge-get-it-done" style that made him invaluable in the years ahead. I could always count on him to speak his mind and give me suggestions and feedback on any issue. The downside to that arrangement was that Wesley would not have a strong vice president for finance until several years later. That meant I had to pay careful attention to that area of operations and perform many of the tasks of a finance officer.

Community Governance

My predecessor brought a collegial mode of administration to the campus. He took an active part in campus affairs and included students, staff and faculty representatives on the newly-created community council. There were two primary committees: the president's committee took care of administrative areas such as housing, food service, parking, campus regulations, and buildings and grounds. The dean's committee, which also included student and staff participation, dealt with degree requirements, curriculum, and expectations of faculty. This bilateral structure provided broad-based participation, but "community governance" required an enormous amount of time and energy. One faculty representative reported there were 17 standing committees and 10 community council committees on which faculty served. He observed that at times, that seemed to be too many committees. He then added that he knew of no way to cut back and still maintain the quality of life and governance which characterized Wesley.

The former president had eight people reporting to him. In 1980, the ATS/MSA accrediting team strongly urged him to reduce that number to three—dean, business manager, and VP for development. The object was to give him more time for external affairs and fundraising. By 1981, his newly-formed administrative council was meeting regularly. That was the senior leadership structure I inherited.

Dean

From the time it was founded in 1882, Wesley never had a dean until 1965, when President Trott appointed L. Harold DeWolf, a distinguished theologian from Boston University. According to lore, that appointment was made without consultation and presented to the faculty as a *fait accompli*. DeWolf brought a wealth of academic experience and a new vision for theological education. That led to a complete revision of Wesley's curriculum and style of preparing students for ministry. He also recruited several new faculty members who had been trained at Boston University. By the time of DeWolf's retirement in 1972, almost half of Wesley's faculty had roots at Boston, prompting quips about Wesley as

"Boston on the Potomac." His successor, J. Philip Wogaman, professor of Christian ethics, was in fact one of the Boston clan.

Six months after I took office, Dean Wogaman told me he wanted to resign at the end of that academic year to invest more time in his research and writing. I managed to catch my breath in time to discuss how we should handle that surprising announcement.

I had a sleepless night. Phil Wogaman, as dean for 10 years, represented stability and continuity in Wesley's academic program. He also suggested that the seminary already had a solid dean candidate within the faculty. Although selecting his replacement from inside would be the quickest and smoothest option, I decided not to choose that option. It did not feel right. Clearly, I did appreciate the seminary's solid academic program, but I wanted to convey a vision that Wesley could be more— an exceptional theological school. My duty was to challenge and guide the seminary toward a changed future.

I talked with Board Chair Wayne Smithey. After his usual grilling, he advised me to follow my instincts and he promised to support whatever decision I made. A few days later I shared with the faculty my vision for Wesley as a leading theological school. I said that we must use every opportunity to challenge ourselves to become the best. We had a good faculty, yes, and we had individuals who could step into the dean's role, but we must look for the best match for our needs, whether we find that leadership from the inside or outside.

I then suggested two steps. First I wanted to have a private, confidential conversation with each faculty member. I wanted to learn about their hopes for

Wesley's future and what kind of leadership we needed from a dean. I also wanted to find out what they wanted and needed from me as president.

Second, I asked them to choose four representatives from among themselves to serve on a search committee. I would then add further committee members from the administration, board, staff and students. We would begin the search as soon as possible, with the goal of having a new dean in fewer than five months.

Those private conversations with the faculty members turned out to be pure gold. I came to a better understanding of what they liked, what they did not like, and what motivated them. They in turn came to a better understanding of what made me tick.

The committee sorted through two dozen resumes before selecting four candidates. One of them was a respected member of the Wesley faculty. He was clearly the sentimental choice of most faculty members. The venerable Clarence Goen advised me to quit acting so presidential and just appoint the person so we could move on. As much as I respected Clarence, I had to tell him I thought that would be a mistake.

The Wesley faculty member was one the two final candidates we called in for interviews. The other was Marjorie Suchochi, who was then a professor and director of the DMin program at Pittsburgh Theological Seminary. Marjorie fairly bubbled over with excitement about theological education, the church, scholarship, teaching, and life in general. She was bright as a new penny and so persuasive that the committee voted for her unanimously. I had the difficult duty of driving out to the faculty member's home to deliver the news in person.

I still remember how heavy my heart was to convey the news.

It was, however, difficult to convince Marjorie to accept the position. As enthusiastically as she presented herself in the interview, she had qualms. She felt too inexperienced. She hated to leave Pittsburgh. She wondered what I would really expect her to do. Would I support her in tough times?

She finally said yes. She still had obligations in Pittsburgh, so we agreed she would come in January. That appointment would make her the first woman academic dean among the 13 United Methodist Theological Schools. She would not only serve Wesley well, but would become influential among the United Methodist schools and in the wider ATS circles. (And Clarence Goen became one of her strongest admirers.)

One of the other candidates posed a challenging question to the committee. Would the dean serve primarily as the representative of the faculty or be primarily a member of the president's leadership team? One of the faculty members said it was the former—the dean, he said, had always been regarded as a member of the faculty, not primarily an administrator.

I felt uneasy with that response, but it did pose a fundamental leadership question. For the past 15 years at least, the dean and faculty had shaped the education program, while the president managed all other administrative areas. Wesley during that period had no serious conflict between the two. My uncase was rooted in my judgment that Wesley had been slightly off track. While virtually everyone would affirm its academic program, very few people knew about Wesley's desperate financial situation and the other educational challenges facing theological schools. We needed a mission and a strategy to address the emerging trends in the world, the church, and theological education. I felt we must address topics such as globalization, the changing nature of seminary student bodies, the decline of Wesley's traditional church constituency, the rising cost of theological education, effective leadership for the church, and many more realities we had yet to identify.

As I continued to reflect on that provocative question in the days ahead, I tried to decide what kind of leadership structure and personnel Wesley would need to meet the oncoming challenges. I believed the president had a mandate from the board to fulfill the seminary's mission and make it sustainable, and all available resources should be focused upon that effort. I believed the senior leadership team should therefore be an extension of the president's office. While the senior officers did have clear areas of responsibility, their work should contribute to the overall mission of the seminary.

In the first year, my work with the senior leadership team was primarily one-to-one with individual members, learning what they were doing and sharing my point of view with them. The team had yet to take on the integrated leadership role that I had in mind for them. Development of that capability would be a gradual process for all concerned, including me.

By the end of that first year, I was pleased with the outstanding group of individuals we had in place—Lovett Weems as vice president, Marjorie Suchocki as dean, Doug Cooney as business manager, and Jim Shopshire as associate dean for student affairs. Every one of them was loaded with talent and deeply committed to the mission of Wesley Seminary. We learned and grew together. We had a good three-year run.

X. Facing the Finances

During the six years of financial decline (fiscal 1976-82), the board's primary emphasis was on raising more money, but it made no specific plan for controlling expenses. Their mantra was: *We have an income problem, not an expense problem.* Those were high inflation years in America. Faced with ever-increasing operating expenses, they still voted 7 percent to 8 percent annual raises for faculty and staff. Unfortunately, the seminary's income did not increase except in the area of church support through the United Methodist Ministerial Education fund (MEF). Those modest increases, however, did not keep pace with rising expenses because the other income areas were not growing. The Centennial Campaign that was launched in 1972 produced less than 20 percent of its $2 million goal. Furthermore, the focus on the campaign had the negative effect of diverting money from the annual fund.

By the fall of 1982, in light of the auditors' warning, the governors did effect some cost controls. With regret, they decided to award no salary increases for 1982-83. They also placed a spending cap of 90 percent on all expense lines in the budget outside of salaries. Then in the summer of 1982, cash flow requirements necessitated an additional loan of $115,000 from the endowment. By the time they met in October of 1982, only $601,762 in invested funds remained in the endowment. They set aside a $20,000 reserve fund for physical-plant emergencies, but prohibited further endowment borrowing without approval of the finance committee.

My financial background was basic. To survive and thrive we—whether a family or an institution—needed more money coming in the door each year than going out. I began to look carefully at each source of the seminary's income and to consider how we could enhance it. The big push, however, focused on fundraising, since everyone assumed that would solve all our fiscal problems. Naively, I thought the same thing. Only later as I began to grasp the overall financial realities of the seminary did I fully realize that adequate income required a balance from several income sources with each area producing its assigned share. Our success in fundraising in the first year and into the future did create a better balance of income. More important, it provided a morale boost for the whole community.

The board also committed itself to help with fundraising. In previous years, almost a quarter of its members made no financial gift. At the fall meeting, all members present committed themselves to make a gift to the annual fund. The financial development committee then organized a solicitation plan by which each member would be called by another member to ask for a gift. Total giving by the board surpassed the $100,000 mark that year for the first time ever.

At the beginning of the 1983-84 fiscal year, the newly-named Committee on Institutional Advancement recommended the following: all board members make an annual gift of at least $1000; all members identify individuals capable of becoming Wesley Council members; and all members consider including Wesley in their estate plan. The board gradually moved toward 100 percent participation in the annual fund, which increased more than 50 percent that first year.

In the spring of 1983, the board also decided to sell the 6 Wesley Circle house and use the proceeds to reduce the debt to the endowment fund.

Success with a Little Luck

With a lot of hard work and some luck that year, we broke the cycle of over-spending. It was more of a field dressing than a cure. We still had some hard times in front of us, but we did a good job. Everyone celebrated. We had set a goal of balancing the budget (1982-83), which meant we had to raise income by $370,000 without spending any more than we did the year before. We managed to expand fundraising by $109,000, which was no mean accomplishment. That still left us with $261,000 to go, which is where the luck came in. I was so focused on fundraising that I had not counted on other areas of income. MEF was up by $182,000, tuition up by $103,000, endowment by $19,000, and auxiliary by $50,000—none of it due to efforts on our part. Altogether, including the fundraising expansion, we increased income by $463 thousand and actually reduced expenses by $42 thousand. We finished with a $54,631 positive balance compared to the dreadful $369,646 deficit the auditors had reported from 1980-81.

The whole Wesley community, including me, was ecstatic and gave all the credit to fundraising. Much later, I realized just how lucky we'd been. Many other fiscal pieces came together that year and helped produce the balanced budget. Whether justified or not, though, I was praised for "saving Wesley." That invested me with enough good will and persuasive power to last for years to come.

There was a downside, of course; there usually is. When all the celebrating was done, we were expected to repeat the miracle every year forevermore. That would take a lot more than luck.

Expenses

We still had the expense side of the budget to address.

 The community's general awareness of Wesley's fiscal dilemma gave me leverage to stress the need to control expenses at every point. That also matched my personal character. My children, since they were teenagers, dubbed me "El Cheapo." They even gave me a personal license plate for my car with El Cheapo on it. The staff who traveled on seminary business had a goal to find a motel cheaper than the president did. Once Lovett Weems and I stayed in a $16 motel room on the Eastern Shore. Lovett loved to recount that the towels and washcloths in our room were so thin he could read the newspaper through them. That record stood for a couple years until one day Chip Aldridge, our director of admissions, rushed into my office one morning and threw a $15 motel receipt on my desk. He confessed that the room was over an all-night bar with blaring music. Chip's record still stands at Wesley today.

The community laughed and teased me, but together we were committed to monitoring our spending and raising more money. Everyone could join in and celebrate our victories whether in fiscal restraint or receiving more gifts. We saved money wherever we could.

As with most seminaries, however, Wesley's most significant expenses were the cost of its educational program and facilities.

When I arrived at the seminary, we had a faculty/student ratio of 1 faculty member for every 8.28 students. Instructional costs were 40 percent of the expense budget. Given Wesley's financial difficulties, I thought that was too high. I wanted to reduce those costs at least modestly. The quality of a seminary education, however, is determined by interaction between faculty and students, which should include a goodly amount of personal attention. My commitment to a high standard of education, shared by the faculty, therefore precluded the reduction of educational expenses. That commitment, in fact, led us to implement so many new and innovative programs over the coming years that by the 1990s, instructional costs had gone up to 48 percent of the expense budget. So much for cutting costs in that area.

We had serious facilities issues hanging over our heads. We needed more library space. We needed to air-condition the Kresge Academic Center. We needed both classroom and office renovations, and we had numerous smaller projects that had been hounding the seminary for more than 10 years. Wesley had tried to do something about all that in the 1970s by launching the campaign that failed so badly. By 1982, the needs had become more pressing than ever, but Wesley was in no condition to launch another campaign to renovate. We had to make sure the boat didn't sink before we began sprucing it up.

A Changing Environment

In 1982, nobody could have foreseen that a tsunami was racing toward the shores of higher education. The most modern piece of office equipment we had back then was an electric typewriter. The PC soon came along to create heretofore unknown educational opportunities; it would also exact a heavy financial toll, just at the time when church support for theological schools began to decline.

For 15 years, Wesley had counted on receiving as much as 30 percent of its income from the annual MEF fund distribution. By 1982, that fell to 26 percent on its way down to the point where we had to make up for the annual loss of some $300,000.

Three sources emerged to fill the gap. One, the endowment grew slowly but steadily, with the annual withdrawal from the endowment moving from 6 percent of the principal to 10 percent. Two, fundraising rose from 8 percent of income in the early 1980s to 17 percent in 2000.

The third income boost came from tuition, but it contained a hidden demon. It had seemed reasonable to keep pace with inflation by raising tuition by 5 percent or so every year. I did not realize those "modest" increases would drive up the cost of education three times faster than the consumer price index. From 1982 through 2001, tuition rose from $95 per credit hour to $345—a shocking increase of 263 percent.

Financial Aid to Students

Wesley allocated 9 percent of its expense budget to financial aid in 1982. Some 18 years later, that percentage was unchanged, which sounds pretty good. When viewed from a different angle, it is more revealing. In 1982, Wesley returned 32 percent of its tuition income in the form of financial aid to students. By 2000, the amount of that financial aid had increased by $473,000— but it was only 22 percent of tuition income.

Those figures make it appear that Wesley was insensitive to the plight of students—not so, by any measure.

Financial aid to students and the growing cost of theological education became one of my primary concerns starting the first day I set foot on campus. The crux of the matter was that just as the students were caught in the grip of a rapidly-changing environment, so was the entire higher-education system in America.

As students looked for ways to meet the higher cost of education, they became increasingly dependent on the Guaranteed Student Loan program. The schools, meanwhile, were also looking for ways to meet their own higher costs. The most readily-available solution—in some cases the *only* available solution—was to raise tuition even more. That vicious cycle piled up a debt load of more than a trillion dollars and cast a pall of gloom over millions of young Americans.

Like so many other schools, Wesley got on that train when it was moving slowly, then couldn't get off when it built up speed. Now—today—a majority of theological students enter a low-paying ministerial workplace with a challenging task of surviving while trying to pay off their loans—plus the accumulating interest and penalties for late payment.

Financial stress in the last two decades of the 20th century spawned an uncountable number of crisis situations for schools and students alike. Many seminaries now find themselves in situations similar to Wesley's in 1982. Whereas we managed to cope with our problems and build a more economically sustainable seminary for the 21st century, it was not without a price. Lovett Weems summed it up this way: *We made debtors out of students and beggars out of presidents.*

XI. Academic Programs and Faculty Development

My academic career began as a chaplain and teacher in a small Methodist college in Tennessee. For three years I taught theology, ethics, and the history of western philosophy, in addition to holding worship services and counseling students. I stayed immersed in other typically academic tasks such as developing new courses, trying to keep one step ahead of students, and grading papers.

I then moved to Chicago to direct an ecumenical project on enlistment for ministry. That was my introduction to seminaries and their issues. During the following three years I worked with several colleagues to create a pilot project in parish development. We teamed up with Protestant and Roman Catholic parishes in the area. The project gave me a first-hand look at the inner workings of pastoral life and pastoral leadership.

The Chicago experience led to a call to Hartford Seminary as a member of a three-person team to develop a totally new, non-degree program there. The seminary had made a dramatic decision to discontinue its degree program, dismiss the entire faculty, and transform itself into a new church-related institution focused on continuing education for pastors, parish development, and research on ministry. That program provided me with the most creative, in-depth educational opportunity of my professional life.

All of this is to say I came to Wesley Seminary in 1982 with a diverse background of teaching, creating new programs, working with parishes, and serving within a theological school. I was therefore surprised by my feelings of ambiguity concerning the faculty and the education program. On the one hand, I wanted to be supportive of the teaching corps. On the other hand, my commitment to the highest possible quality of theological education meant some changes had to be made. Most people don't like change, especially when it means loss of a job. For starters, we already had too many faculty members for the size of our student body.

Providentially, three senior members were about to retire, and one part-time member in music was coming up for tenure. Through discussions with the dean and the faculty personnel committee, we decided to replace the part-time member with an adjunct. As for the three positions that would need replacements, we decided not to fill one for an undetermined period and let the other two stand vacant for one year. The dean also cancelled four courses that had been taught by adjuncts. Those savings would give us time to consider what we needed and what we could afford going forward. I felt good about the process we used to make those hard decisions. The faculty as a body also agreed with the recommendations.

The college of hard knocks had found a new way to teach me yet another lesson. Mary Alice Edwards marched into my office while I was sitting there feeling good about the cost reductions. She was one of the faculty members who would be retiring, and she had clout. Mary Alice had been the first woman awarded tenure in the history of Wesley Seminary. She was highly respected, known as an excellent teacher with a warm heart and a gentle demeanor—although not gentle at that particular moment.

Without pausing to sit, she said, "President Lewis, if you do not fill my position when I retire, then I will not retire."

I tried to explain that her position would be vacant only for one year, but—

"Not acceptable! Without two faculty positions, our Christian education program will fail. I will not stand for that."

She marched out as resolutely as she had marched in. We filled her position. She retired.

I had already discerned that my presidential powers were not absolute. That lesson served as a reminder that sometimes it is prudent to back up, reverse course, and develop a whole new strategy.

XII. Learning About Planning

Clearly, Wesley needed to have a plan, and it was up to me to see to that. I had always been a planner by nature, thinking about the future whether for myself, my family, or any group in which I was a participant. I wanted to know where we were going and how to get there.

The Association of Theological Schools and Middle States Association accrediting teams had visited Wesley's campus in the spring of 1981 to assess and make recommendations concerning Wesley's accreditation status in the two associations. The team had recommended that Wesley be continued in its accredited status. However, it made strong recommendations concerning the seminary's financial situation, its administrative structure, and its lack of a long-range plan to extricate itself from such a precarious position. They further required that a team from the associations make a follow-up visit in the fall of 1982 to evaluate the progress.

I was surprised by the follow-up visit and did not know what to expect. The visiting committee quickly conveyed its concern about Wesley's financial situation but seemed satisfied that we were getting a grasp on the problem. Team members affirmed the significant new efforts we were making in fundraising. They also were laudatory about my commitment and progress in assembling a strong and effective senior leadership team and our style of working together.

One of their team members, the president of Gettysburg College, met with me privately. He said it was obvious to the committee that we had no formal planning process underway. He pressed me concerning my knowledge about strategic planning and how I intended to lead a planning process at Wesley Seminary. Inasmuch as I did not know the meaning of "strategic planning," I struggled to avoid intimidation. How, I wondered, was that different from plain old planning? No doubt sensing my unease, my grand inquisitor graciously shifted into the role of mentor. For the next hour he described his own experience learning about the planning process they used at Gettysburg College and the benefits it produced.

I got the message and immediately began "planning how to plan." When the board held its winter meeting, I reported my intention of developing a plan that would guide us through the next several years.

Planning to Plan

I spent a considerable amount of time learning about planning during the first three-quarters of 1983. I spoke with people holding leadership positions in other schools and with consultants as well. It became evident that we should make a comprehensive assessment of all aspects of the seminary. We had many issues facing us, and it was important that we understand them clearly before we could address them effectively.

I hired a planning consultant. I set up a planning committee with myself as co-chair paired with board member Helen Smith. We formed a steering committee with representatives from the board, faculty, administration, staff, students, and alumni. The seminary community responded with enthusiasm, as evidenced by the appearance of Lash Gwynn at the first meeting of the steering committee. Lash had agreed to be a staff representative. Although he worked as a cataloger in the library, he dressed like an old mountain man or possibly the sidekick in a cowboy movie. When he showed up wearing a coat and tie and proceeded to make thoughtful contributions, that told me our wheels were on the right track. He had a perfect attendance record throughout the project.

The inauguration of the planning committee was January, 1984. Its work continued through May of 1985 with countless meetings involving dozens of individuals and seminary committees throughout the year. That first major effort taught me a lot about institutional planning and the essential role a president plays in the process. It also introduced a planning culture within the seminary, a dividend of no small significance.

Leadership and Change: A President's Story

Phase II

A Gradual Turn

1985-1990

I. A New Long-Range Plan

II. Role of Space for Community and Education

III. Academic Program Development in the 80s

IV. Building a Diverse Community

V. Enrollment

VI. Senior Administrative Team

VII. Building the Board of Governors

VIII. Fundraising/Institutional Advancement

IX. Financial Management

X. Care and Development of a President

I. A New Long-Range Plan

Phase I had seen us right our educational ship. Then we gradually shifted to making it seaworthy. Our first step was to itemize the needs of each facet of the seminary and arrange those in order of priority. Once that was done, we were able to set a course to reach Wesley's long-term goals.

We devised a plan that would guide us for the remainder of the 1980s. It was not a simple task, for it had to encompass issues of educational capacity, facilities, personnel, support constituency, financial resources, governance, leadership, and more.

I had ideas and visions about what the seminary should do and how to go about it. However, I did not believe a good president should (or even could) simply issue proclamations; there were numerous viewpoints to consider. Wesley had a long-held tradition of shared decision-making, and many people who cared deeply about it: the board, the staff, students, the church constituency, and countless external forces. Even so, the seminary had chosen me to lead. I was expected to choose the tune and call the dance. What I was not expected to do was choose the wrong music or call the wrong steps—no rock and roll when a waltz was preferred.

I suggested a long-range planning process that would involve representatives from all parts of the institution, as well as an outside consultant for objective guidance. The board of governors had awarded me high marks for our Phase I success, which translated into the confidence and good will of the overall Wesley community. That gave me the necessary leverage to serve as co-chair of the planning committee. In that capacity, I had a first-hand look at all input from the five subcommittees and thus could insert my ideas directly into the process.

With more than a year of planning work behind it, our committee presented this summary of its final plan to the board of governors in May of 1985:

EXCELLENCE IN MINISTRY

A Vision for Wesley Theological Seminary

Excellence in ministry is the goal of Wesley Seminary. Our mission is to serve the church through preparing its leaders and providing theological leadership on issues facing the church and the world. Surviving as an institution and preserving the status quo is not enough. We must strive to be the best our potential will allow, and our potential is great. We have an unmatched location, a superior and growing faculty and the capability of drawing a first-rate student body. We are located in an area with a strong United Methodist history as well as a large contemporary membership, but we are also ecumenical in spirit and in the makeup of faculty, student body and constituency. We draw students regionally, nationally, and internationally.

Taking cognizance of our location in the nation's capital in the center of much of the world's political power, we have committed ourselves to train people for ministry with a global perspective and to be a resource to the church on issues of theology and public policy.

Preparation for ministry is not an easy task. It requires behavioral, spiritual, and intellectual development. We believe that this is best accomplished in a collegial, communal setting which promotes intellectual inquiry and theological reflection, nourishes individuals, teaches accountability, integrates learning, and promotes worship and community building.

Framework

The plan was divided into five major areas with a task force assigned to each:
   1) Curriculum and Program
   2) External Affairs and Institutional Advancement
   3) Student Services and Community Life
   4) Facilities and Equipment
   5) Finance

Each task force concentrated on these factors as they applied to their particular area:
   a) clarification of mission
   b) a baseline data study
   c) forecasting
   d) visioning
   e) proposing plans to achieve their vision

These in-depth reports were presented to the board along with the summary. However, they were mainly used as guidance in the follow-up work during the next few years.

Objectives

In order to pursue excellence in ministry and to continue to fulfill our potential as a theological school, Wesley in the next few years must:

- Commit itself to seeking and attracting candidates of the highest quality
- Support and develop a faculty of increasing excellence to provide first-rate educational programs that are ecclesial in focus

- Extend our educational resources to clergy and to laity in ministry
- Increase Wesley's theological leadership on issues facing the church and the world
- Improve our physical facilities and provide an aesthetically pleasing environment which promotes creativity

The means of achieving these objectives were spelled out in detail in the stated goals and objectives for each of the five areas of our long-range plan.

<u>Vision and Realism</u>

Any good planning process will generate tension between a lofty vision and what is realistically possible. Our long-range planning project was no exception. It challenged Wesley to become one of the leading theological schools in America. It then detailed the steps to take and the resources needed to achieve that vision.

The steps:

- Increase our permanent financial resources through endowed professorships and scholarships for student aid
- Expand our learning resources, such as library space and materials and other state-of-the-art educational resources
- Improve and refurbish some of our physical facilities
- Initiate a capital campaign to raise $5.1 million to fund the goals

These challenging goals would require sacrificial support and new levels of leadership from our board of governors, faculty, staff, and friends. In addition, it would require attracting, challenging, and involving new friends for Wesley. Together we wanted to move Wesley to new heights of leadership and service for the church.

President's Goals

At the March, 1985 meeting of the executive committee of the board as part of my evaluation, I presented my goals for the year:

1. Complete our long-range plan
2. Continue to build my leadership team
3. Continue to expand our constituency (key leadership people)
4. Solicit major gifts in our endowment program
5. Continue development of the board of governors and the president's advisory council
6. Balance the budget
7. Expand new programs
8. Teach one course annually
9. Continue my personal and professional growth by participating in the Theological Educational Management Program

Fruitful Planning

Planning is a never-ending process. It functions best as a continuing mode of evaluating the present and visioning a new and more creative future. In any institution, subterranean issues always exist, and they require long-term vision and steady, persistent work if they are to serve the institution well and not undermine it. Our early planning efforts as a seminary community helped us reaffirm our deepest values and establish common goals. It also made us aware of the challenges that lay in our path to making Wesley the theological institution we envisioned.

A president needs the whole community to understand the mission of the school and commit to the strategic goals necessary to fulfill a vision for its future. On the other hand, a president has special duties that only the leader can carry out in each area. This balancing act requires a partnership with members of the community.

Reflecting on the seminary's life and work, I began to understand these deeper-level issues and how the seminary struggled with them and was ultimately shaped by them. Some of these issues existed at the time of my arrival and others cropped up later. Whatever their source or duration, they required my attention in order to integrate them into the life and mission of the seminary.

II. Role of Space for Community and Education

In 1958, Westminster Theological Seminary moved from Westminster, Maryland, to Washington, D.C., and became Wesley Theological Seminary. The same architectural style was apparent in all five of the newly-constructed buildings, which included one for administration (with a chapel), one for education, a library, a 66-room dormitory, and a house for the president. An apartment dorm for married students was added in 1966.

Wesley's beautiful nine-acre campus in the heart of Washington had been property of The American University (AU) right next door. AU was founded by the Methodist Church and its continuing close relationship to the church was reflected in the amount it charged Wesley for the land—10 dollars. The seminary purchased its utilities from the university, and Wesley students were provided access to its library, courses, and athletic facilities. Wesley faculty and staff families enjoyed tuition remission at the university. Over time, some joint degree programs were also developed.

G. Bromley Oxnam, the Methodist bishop of the Washington area during the 1950s, served as chair of the boards of Wesley and AU. His vision of a strong Methodist presence in Washington and his skillful use of ecclesiastical power facilitated the seminary's move and fostered the close university-seminary relationship. The seminary chapel is named for him, and his ashes rest under its altar.

From the beginning, there had been talk of the seminary eventually becoming a part of the university, but that merger never came to fruition. Some say Bishop Oxnam did not remain in office long enough to complete a full merger. In any case, a strong resolve always existed among the Wesley faculty and board to be closely related to AU while maintaining Wesley's institutional independence. Over the years, various administrators at AU even raised the issue of Wesley Seminary becoming one of the schools of the university. The president of AU during one of my first meetings with him posed that possibility and talked about the advantages for the university and the seminary.

Frankly, I was never inclined to encourage a Wesley move in that direction. Though I appreciated the benefits of our relationship with AU, I felt Wesley's mission was better served as an independent theological school than as one of the schools of a university.

Bishop Oxnam was not only persuasive in church and academic communities but in the financial world as well. He convinced Sebastian Kresge and his son Stanley to donate half of the $3 million construction costs for the new campus. The Wesley board and its president, Norman Trott, raised the other $1.5 million, which made it possible for the new seminary to start out with no mortgage obligations.

A Growing Clamor About Space Issues

Within a decade of its move to Washington, the seminary began to experience pressing needs for more space. The library collection had grown significantly and filled most of the available shelves even as the students cried out for more private-study carrels. The education building and the dormitory were acutely uncomfortable during Washington's famously hot months—neither of them had air-conditioning. Standing three stories high with no elevators, they were not handicap-accessible.

There was also an increasing number of complaints about poor lighting and lack of adequate furniture in classrooms and offices. These obvious needs, along with the cost of regular building maintenance, replacement of basic equipment, and expansion of the library had prompted the seminary to launch a financial campaign during the 1970s.

Because the campaign failed, the same list of space issues, plus others, sat heavily upon my desk when I arrived in 1982. During my first two years, little could be done. We struggled financially just to keep up with day-to-day operations. Our first priority was staying alive as an institution.

My awareness of the critical and complex nature of space issues increased with each passing day. Location, land, buildings, and maintenance were important but also multidimensional and systemic. Since each space can have multiple uses, individual members of the community therefore contend for them. There needed to be an equitable method of prioritizing. The educational program itself, and the nature of the student body should and would influence the special needs for space, its design, and affordability.

Changing times intensified the situation. When Wesley opened its new campus in 1958 with 143 students, most of them were young white males with a majority expected to live in Straughn Hall. They would eat in the refectory that served meals during the week. Classrooms were basically lecture halls. Worship was in a traditional chapel —pews only. All members of the administration and faculty had adequate office space.

By 1982, however, Wesley had more than 350 students, most of whom lived off-campus. As commuters, they needed places to study and to relax between classes, and some needed overnight accommodations once or twice a week. Parking became more important than dorm space.

The number of faculty and staff had almost doubled since 1958. Wesley now had a bookstore, and new centers had emerged—Arts and Religion, Theology and Public Policy, Lay Resource Center—all of which needed room to function. Office space was at a premium; some faculty offices had been moved into the dormitory. These new demands joined the still unresolved issues of library, air-conditioning, and accessibility, along with a newly-discovered asbestos problem. The community had of necessity coped with these situations as best they could, but nobody was happy about it.

Faced with such intensifying problems and a lack of funds to solve them, the temptation was to fix a few of the most pressing needs and hope that would placate most of the community. For almost 20 years the seminary had practiced a "strategy of postponement." The capital campaign of the 1970s had produced only enough for bandages on small abrasions, but the larger wounds had been left to fester untreated.

The long-range planning work that began in 1984 addressed these needs and their importance to Wesley's future. Considerable funding would be required to make the plan work, which pointed to another fundraising campaign. The sad results of the previous campaign, however, did not impart a sense of optimism about such an idea. We simply had to find a better way to get the job done.

Tom Broce came to the rescue. As our development consultant, he earned his keep by proposing a novel strategy called the "40 percent share" goal. He reasoned that a campaign target announced to the public from day one might prove unattainable and thus produce another failure. He suggested that we first approach selected potential donors and ask for their pledges discretely. That would allow us to get a sense of what we might reasonably expect to accomplish. The sum of those initial pledges would then become 40 percent of the final goal.

Tom's idea worked in spectacular fashion. Neither Westminster nor Wesley had ever experienced financial commitments of such caliber, and it started with a bang that shocked and excited the board members. The initial pledges of the campaign committee put $600,000 dollars on the table before the campaign even started. For the first time in its history, the board had grasped a long range plan and the commitment of resources to see it through.

Confidence in the capital campaign grew out of the seminary's financial turnaround since 1982. Optimism filled the air as I shared these numbers with the board:

Operating Fund	1981	1982	1983	1984	1985
Rev. over Expense	(156,011)	(369,366)	54,361	155,561	76,003
Due to Other Funds	653,088	1,023,712	754,335	626,255	254,046
Fund Balance	(565,357)	(944,723)	(621,222)	(340,660)	(76,320)

Endowment Fund	1981	1982	1983	1984	1985
	1,375,394	762,023	1,487,796	2,009,873	3,238,657

Looking back, the figures do not appear dramatic. However, for a Wesley community that had only known depressing financial numbers for several years, they had the effect of an elixir.

Focus of Presidential Leadership

During this period I focused on three essential leadership functions:

1. Help the community understand and define the reality of its setting
2. Identify critical issues that need to be addressed by the community
3. Generate a vision for addressing these issues

Virtually everyone related to the seminary could talk about its history, its relationship to AU, its location in Washington, and the blessings of our campus. They also knew what needed to be fixed, changed, or added. They even knew the limits of the seminary's financial resources. What they did *not* know was how to put all the pieces of the puzzle together and pose a realistic vision.

I had suggested a long-range planning process and pushed the idea that together we could and would come to a deeper understanding of the reality of Wesley at that moment. We could dream up new possibilities for its future, too. But first we had to roll up our sleeves and get serious. The board had to face up to the seminary's financial needs realistically and provide quality leadership. We had two new board members—Barbara Kettler-Mills and Bill Klinedinst—who kick-started that transformation. Their willingness to commit themselves and their financial resources generated excitement that unlocked the energy and generosity of the other board members and the wider community.

Finally, I recognized that we should not approach the spatial issues piecemeal. We needed a comprehensive picture of all the issues, and a detailed plan to address them in bold fashion.

A Space-Usage Study

My recommendation was to begin with a study of how Wesley was utilizing its space. The board authorized that study in February of 1986. We considered four companies and settled on Celentano-Esposito. The building and grounds committee instructed Bob Esposito to study our long-range plan, our existing facilities, and our current usage. From those results we could then project a future usage plan.

The space-study and plan was completed by the end of the summer, 1986. At the October board meeting, the chair of the building and grounds committee, Isham Baker, reviewed the major features of the study. I followed him with a walk-through of the building diagrams to explain the suggested changes in further detail. Instead of recommending new buildings, we chose to focus on renovation of the library and the academic center (Kresge) at a projected cost of $2.06 million. The faculty representative to the board reported that faculty members had been consulted on all aspects of the project and had given their strong endorsement.

The board approved. The finance committee was to work out the financing details—not to exceed the amount raised in the capital campaign. Very soon thereafter, that would all seem like the easy part; we had months of disruptive construction ahead of us.

Regrettably, because of funds limitations, we had to bypass renovating Straughn Hall. For the next 20 years it would soldier on without central air-conditioning or an elevator or improved bathroom arrangements. But that was reality.

We got blindsided by one issue that could not have been anticipated. Our buildings were constructed during the 1950s, when plaster was laced with asbestos. Now, a great stir rose up concerning the dangerous effects of asbestos fibers. We spent considerable time and more than a quarter of a million dollars on that situation before it became known that asbestos is harmful only when disturbed. We replaced it in the areas where construction took place, but left it untouched everywhere else.

Managing the Process

I gave thanks daily for having convinced Doug Cooney to become Wesley's business manager. As such, he assumed the duties of monitoring and managing the building and grounds during the construction project. His cheerful spirit, commitment to details, and pursuit of excellence made all of us feel comfortable and confident of the project's ultimate success.

As essential as the renovation was, I had never been involved in such a complicated and disruptive endeavor. In the beginning, I questioned whether I should focus on the big picture or be concerned about the most important of the many details that were involved. Gradually, I came to understand that I had to do both.

I also needed to keep the community aware of what we were trying to achieve. The problems had been swept under the rug for too many years, and our duty was to set things on track. We could only achieve what we could afford, but I had a vision beyond just the restoration of a status quo. I wanted our newly-renovated facilities not only to function better, but to look and *feel* better. I wanted a place that would inspire individuals to reflect more deeply about themselves and their community. I wanted a place that would inspire groups of individuals to be more open with each other and to face challenging issues with courage and determination. I wanted us to create something that would reflect the spirit of Wesley Seminary and instill pride in our hearts and those of future generations.

I did not quite know what this vision would look like or how to go about its creation, but I did know that I would recognize it when it appeared. Faculty member Larry Rasmussen said I wanted space that would be "aesthetically precious." He nailed it.

As though in answer to my wishes, we received a surprise gift of $100,000 from Arthur and Marjorie Dadian for the purpose of building an art gallery. That was both fortuitous and challenging. Although it would be small, it should be exquisite. But who knew how to design such an edifice? Where could we put it? Where *should* we put it?

After considerable discussion, we decided the gallery should be in a place that was adjacent to a primary meeting place for the Wesley community. It would greet people as they walked from the central courtyard into Kresge's main entrance. That would necessitate moving one or two faculty offices as well as redesigning Elderdice Hall.

The gallery design was contentious from the outset. The architect's initial proposal had the look of a storefront. Catherine Kapikian and the new gallery curator were horrified. Catherine said that neither Washington nor Wesley needed an art gallery with a shopping-mall mentality. The architect did not take especially well to that criticism. Finally, I put my foot down. I herded Catherine, the curator, and the architect into one room and told them none of us could leave until we had a new design that satisfied everybody. Several hours later, we emerged with an extraordinary design that combined beauty, flexibility, and practicality. The gallery, which would host dozens of shows in the coming years, would set the tone for the entire building.

The final design proved more expensive than our original budget, but I supported the overrun. I believed that a bit of presidential persuasion with the board members would get an okay—which it did.

The renovation brought up numerous yes-no decisions I would have to make. Many were of small import, but each one had conflicting advocates with strong opinions. One senior professor demanded that his office should be one foot longer than his associate. Why? He said it was because he had greater responsibilities than his associate. It was not difficult to veto that request. Other suggestions, such as a central space for a student lounge, got my yes-vote immediately.

Construction of educational spaces began after spring semester in May of 1988. The schedule called for them to be finished before the fall term began, but that did not happen. It is common knowledge that most construction projects fall behind; ours fell seriously behind. Thanks in part to a plumbing problem, the disruption dragged on through the fall semester. We had to close the refectory and the library during some of the work.

The solution to the library space became compact shelving that tripled the shelf space for the book collection and freed up other space for study areas and special collections. It required taking over a room in the basement of the Trott Administration Building which connected underground to the library.

Some members of the faculty complained that we were appropriating too much educational space for other purposes.

The Courtyard and the Rains

One of the board members, Barbara Kettler-Mills, insisted that——we should also renovate the seminary's nondescript courtyard, which linked the seminary's three main buildings. She backed up her judgment with a gift that paid for the renovation, including a new design. That work began in the spring of 1989.

That spring was a wet one for Washington. Bulldozers and the rains turned the courtyard into a soggy mud-hole. One morning a staff member came rushing into my office proclaiming a bulldozer was about to plow into the second floor of the administration building. I rushed outside to discover a mound of dirt that reached the second level of the building. A bulldozer was right on top of the pile pushing more dirt, higher and higher toward

81

the building. It did not, of course, drive into the building, but it looked that way to those of us who knew nothing about the moving of dirt.

We had a torrential rain on the Friday before Monday's graduation ceremonies. It flooded the courtyard and rushed into the still-unfinished elevator shaft of the Kresge Building. Staff member Randall Adams and I, along with a few students, started bailing. We labored all afternoon and into the evening, but we could not prevail over Mother Nature. That frantic effort earned me the title "Chair of the Bucket Brigade."

Early that Saturday morning I walked up from our house to review the situation. The shaft had indeed filled and overflowed into the refectory. The entire dining room lay under several inches of water. With a graduation lunch and reception scheduled there within 48 hours, I felt helpless and hopeless. In desperation I called the Saunders brothers, Fred and Peter. Those two Englishmen had worked on the seminary grounds crew for the past 20 years. They lived 80 miles away, but without a word of protest they heeded my call. Two hours later they arrived with a water vacuum in the back of their pickup and worked all weekend. By Monday they had the refectory ready for business, and graduation proceeded without a hitch. In my book the Saunders brothers deserved a statue alongside John Wesley on his horse.

The president's house, down the hill from the main seminary buildings, did not escape the marauding spring rainwater. American University had decided to expand the drainage capacity of the underground pipes that carry all the drainage water from the campus into the city's storm-water system. That 36-inch pipe ran across the backyard of the president's house. Heavy rains would periodically cause it to flood our backyard. On this occasion the flood flowed into the basement and inundated our cars in the parking lot.

There was a house under construction across the street from ours. The lot contained several huge granite rocks that had to be broken up for removal. The sound of dynamite going off at various intervals, unannounced, teamed up with floods, mud, and delays made it a frustrating time for the Wesley seminary community and especially the president's family.

When school started in the fall of 1989, the Wesley campus had a distinctively different look about it. From an educational standpoint, it was more functional, and it imparted that special feel I had wanted and trusted would be recognized. During the next 20 years, we continued with small renovation ventures and ran a tight maintenance ship, but we undertook no major projects. Later, under David McAllister-Wilson's leadership, Wesley built a magnificent new 85-bed dormitory and undertook major redesign and renovation of the chapel, library, and Straughn Hall.

Information Technology

The total number of computers on the Wesley campus in 1982 came to zero. The computer age then swept over us, starting in the administrative offices. By 1988, thanks to a generous grant from Lilly Endowment, we furnished a PC for each faculty member. Gradually, we expanded our capacity in all the offices and entered the modern digital age.

Higher education made significant investments in information technology during the ensuing years, Wesley included. This phenomenon, along with multiple other new expenses—complying with ever-increasing governmental regulations, cost of living increases, additional staffing, facilities, scholarships, etc.—escalated the cost of education across the country. Education was challenged to search for increased revenue and ultimately struggled to create new financial models that would enable them to remain viable into the new century.

New Management

Bob Greene and his wife Caroline retired in 1984 after a quarter-century of service at Wesley. Bob was manager of buildings and grounds. Caroline worked in various administrative offices. An era had come to its end, for they were the last of those who had moved from Westminster to Washington in the late 1950s.

From a personal standpoint, I was delighted by their excitement about retirement. From a professional standpoint, I feared finding their replacements would not be an easy task. The business manager at American University suggested we consider AU's method. They had a contract with a nationwide facilities-management company called Service Masters. After deliberations, we arranged to have that company place a manager on our campus. He would be under the guidance and supervision of the on-site manager at AU. That seemed like a good plan at the time, one that would suit our needs and bring us into an even closer relationship with AU.

Two years later, we contracted to have Service Masters provide us with our own manager of buildings and grounds, reporting directly to our business manager. A few years after that, we hired our own B&G manager. That turned out to be a wise decision, thanks to her loyalty and the personal touch she brought to our small community.

I never directly supervised the manager of B&G, but I kept up with what was going on. Any decision about larger repairs and renovations always came to my desk. One practice that I started early and continued throughout my tenure was to take a detailed, guided tour of every aspect of the grounds and facilities every year. That tour and occasional informal conversations with the manager and members of the crew kept me abreast of the issues. It also assured our B&G manager that she was free to approach me whenever on any issue.

As with most institutions, there was always back-channel, insider information. In this case it would flow through Shirley, my wife, who knew the grounds crew very well. After all, our yard was part of the seminary grounds, and our house was one of its buildings. They liked her and felt comfortable talking with her. In many informal conversations they would share their insider information about what was "really happening" on the campus. Sometimes it was their way of sending a message to the president without risking a direct conversation with me. I actually learned a lot of important information through that avenue of communication, but I always had to weigh it against other information that came my way.

III. Academic Program Development in the 1980s

Marjorie Suchocki moved into the position of academic dean in January of 1983, full of energy and ideas. Having never served as a dean, she wanted to make an immediate impact. What better to way to do that, she reasoned, than to revise the curriculum

I agreed with her that a thorough review and redesign of the curriculum was called for. Significant changes were taking place in the church's ministries and the student body. The world faced a daunting array of new issues—information technology, globalization, and social changes in the society. I therefore supported her initiative and urged her to bring the faculty into the process. The faculty, in fact, was very open to the new challenge and wanted to work with their new dean.

By the beginning of the fall semester, the dean and the faculty had formed a committee to lead the curriculum revision. Bruce Birch, Professor of Old Testament, served as chair of the committee, working with Marjorie. Bruce was a skillful and thoughtful educator. The committee, with participation from most of the faculty, worked throughout the year that followed. It focused on data-gathering and ministry study during the fall and put forth an intense effort that spring to devise the new curriculum design. They kept the academic affairs committee of the board informed, and finally brought the revised curriculum to the board at its meeting in May of 1985. In presenting it to the board, the dean said the new curriculum might well represent a breakthrough in theological education. She felt the accomplishment was a witness to the collegiality and intellectual strengths of the faculty.

The new proposed curriculum represented a dramatic change in the seminary's MDiv and MRE programs. It had two distinct features: (a) an ecclesial focus and (b) an integration of academic disciplines into the core courses. Marjorie expressed it this way: "We study from *within* the church, *for* the church, and *with* the church."

During each of its first two years, the new design required a two-semester core course—*Introduction to the Church and Her Ministries*. The first year introduced students to the global and local church in its various dimensions—theological, sociological, liturgical, and

86

missional. It was team-taught by several faculty members during the semester. That arrangement was later reinforced by having smaller numbers of students meet in reflection groups. The second year paired theology and ethics and a two-semester experience of a covenant-discipleship group, modeled after John Wesley's class band system. The third year required a small-group seminar focused on the students writing a major paper integrating theoretical and practical material from all their previous work.

The new design necessitated an increased effort from faculty in preparation, team teaching, and personal work with individual students. The system proceeded well enough during the 1980s, but changing times eventually caused it to fray at the edges. This integrating-teaching required more time from faculty and did not allow as much focus on each member's area of academic discipline and interest. The greatest resistance, though, came from the students. While not opposed to the integrative focus or emphasis on the church, they had a problem with logistics. The makeup of the student body had changed. More part-time students had enrolled, and it was inconvenient for many of them to attend class except during the evening.

The core course was scheduled in the daytime on Thursdays, with little flexibility. As if that were not a sufficiently difficult state of affairs, the part-timers could not keep in sync with the three-year structure. We responded to their needs and built in more flexibility, including a return to more traditional required courses (e.g. Old Testament, New Testament, Church History, Theology, etc.) that students could work into their demanding schedules.

The new curriculum did bring forth a new commitment for Wesley. The seminary intentionally declared itself to be church-focused in its educational program. That commitment would become even more evident in the 1990s. The faculty also redesigned the DMin program. It was meant to be an in-depth continuing education-and-renewal period for pastoral ministers. The first year consisted of a nucleus of required courses covering basic areas. In the second year, a pastor could select four elective courses in an area of his/her interest. Third-year students selected an issue in their ministries, developed a method for working on it, and finally reported on it in a project thesis.

The structure for the basic track was one day a week for three 11-week periods covering the six basic courses. For the first time, Wesley also offered a concentrated (week intensives) version of the same program. This alternative opened the door to more flexible designs later, and shaped how Wesley would offer the DMin degree in the future.

A Church Focus

As an extension of this new church focus and integration of academic and ministry praxis, we invited the bishop and representatives of the cabinet from the three contiguous annual conferences around Wesley—Baltimore/Washington, Peninsula, and Virginia—for a day's consultation on the Wesley campus. We discussed the curriculum and how we could work together in preparing students for leadership in the church's ministries. This time together enhanced our partnership, trust, and cooperative efforts with these key conferences. It reminded the seminary and its faculty of whom we served. It also increased the conferences' knowledge and support of Wesley's educational philosophy and programs.

Concretely, it generated support and facilitation for a new student pastor track in our MDiv program. The conferences committed to make four-year pastoral appointments to selected Wesley students who would be admitted to the four-year student pastor track. This program—enrolling about 15 students per year—proved enormously successful in preparing an individual for pastoral ministry. It has remained active now for more than 20 years. At the same time, we initiated an urban ministry track based on the same educational model. It never attracted as many students, but it did affirm Wesley's commitment to the city and to urban ministry.

Effectiveness in Ministry

No seminary can guarantee that a student will be effective in ministry, but it is duty-bound to try. It starts with recruitment, with finding excellent candidates. That is a complex issue. What defines excellence? Who defines excellence? What is required to prepare someone for effective leadership? How will ongoing support be provided?

Sad to say, the church's selection process is complicated and inefficient. It has been a long-standing bone of contention between seminaries and denominations whose students attend those seminaries. The ongoing nurturing and growth of pastors are also managed inadequately by the institutional church. Very few Protestant denominations cooperate directly with seminaries in recruiting individuals, preparing them for their future ministry, or sustaining them throughout their careers. If the results of those inadequacies prove disappointing, it is all too easy for them to blame the seminary.

Wesley reached out to its nearby United Methodist judicatories and affirmed its commitment to work together as closely as possible. We emphasized that Wesley was of and for the church. We strived to better coordinate and integrate with these conferences the process of preparing candidates for the church's ministries, and emphasized that should be an ongoing process. We would continue that philosophy and that commitment. However, we felt the need to make a shift in how we related to the church in our area during the 1990s. That part of the story comes later.

New Program Elements

Some elements of the curriculum revision would continue even as the core design evolved in the ensuing years. An awareness of global issues and the world church changed forms but continued as an integral part of the curriculum. Wesley's participation in the Plowshares Globalization of Theological Education Project and the Palestine Awareness Program provided opportunities for faculty, board, and administrators to experience immersion trips to various parts of the world. These experiences had such powerful and consciousness-changing effects that the faculty subsequently instituted a cross-cultural immersion as a requirement for all MDiv students.

The Arts

The little gallery made possible by the Dadians turned out to be a seed that grew into figurative vines that entwined themselves around the hearts of the Wesley community. The arts not only became part of the environment, they became part of the curriculum for a master's degree from the seminary. Each student would now be required to take one course in the arts. The offerings expanded to include the visual arts, music, dance, drama, and poetry.

Ministry to the Hearing-Impaired

The Washington area had one of the largest populations of hearing-impaired individuals in America, partly due to Gallaudet College. A number of congregations for hearing-impaired individuals also existed in the Washington area. Some were United Methodist. The denomination, concerned about preparing pastors for these churches, provided support and encouragement for Wesley to create a special program for these potential pastors. The seminary's investment included a part-time faculty person to teach and manage the program and a person who would sign for certain courses. Regrettably we had to discontinue the program after four years because church funding declined, and the program never attracted more than six people.

Social Issues Retreats

Early in my tenure we sponsored a racism workshop for board members, faculty, and staff. The students insisted that we follow up with another one for them. That worked out so well that it led us to plan an annual Social Issues Awareness weekend workshop. The topics rotated from racism, sexism, drugs and alcohol, to sexuality. Every student was required to attend at least two of the workshops. They had a powerful impact on the Wesley community and stirred numerous conversations. We had calls for particular actions, and in some case frustration and anger on the part of students who thought the seminary was not doing enough in a particular area. In one sense the workshops provoked more energy and demand than the seminary was equipped to handle. After five or six years they slowly faded from the community.

We generally concluded that it was a good idea whose time had expired.

Chair in Evangelism

In 1981, the Foundation for Evangelism announced a new signature program—the E. Stanley Jones Professors of Evangelism. Its primary goal was to encourage and help fund a Professor of Evangelism in each of the United Methodist seminaries. The director of the foundation, Charles Kinder, had graduated from Wesley and was anxious to establish a chair there. He approached me with a proposal to assist in endowing a chair with a commitment of funds raised by his foundation. His offer provoked interest on our part, until two problems cropped up.

First, the foundation had a narrow definition of evangelism, which included how it should be taught in a seminary. Second, the foundation staff wanted to retain the right to veto any faculty candidate chosen by the seminary according to a long-established process of selection. Our faculty rejected the foundation's offer out of hand, as did all other United Methodist seminaries. I considered the issue dead.

I later received word that recently-retired Bishop Earl Hunt had become the new director of the foundation. He had been a distinguished pastor in the Holston Conference, which was my home conference. It was also the home conference of Jim Logan, one of the most respected members of the Wesley faculty. Bishop Hunt sought our counsel in re-opening the issue of a chair at Wesley. He, Jim, and I put our heads together and through a series of meetings and calls hammered out a new contractual agreement that proved satisfactory to all of the UM seminaries. The door was thus opened for Wesley to have an E. Stanley Jones Professor of

Evangelism. Funding for the first three years came from the foundation and a layman of the Virginia conference—B.B. Lane, who had also been a donor to Wesley. It was agreed that at the end of those three years, Wesley and the Foundation for Evangelism would share the cost of the faculty member.

Fortune smiled on us again when Jim Logan indicated that he was willing to step into that evangelism professorship. During the next decade, he planted evangelism firmly into the Wesley curriculum as well as the hearts and minds of the students. That good fortune extended to the foundation too, for Jim proved himself to be a tremendous asset in establishing similar professorships in other UM schools. He also helped guide the Foundation for Evangelism through a process of moderating its position vis-à-vis relations with other seminaries and other projects.

Presidential Involvement

I found myself in the midst of a number of experiments in education. We struggled to integrate them into basic programs in a manner that addressed our core mission, which was to prepare students for leadership in church ministries. I was usually the final arbiter of what we would do with this array of educational options. I struggled often for relevant criteria with which to reach proper decisions. Many factors came into play. Was the proposal educationally sound and productive? Would it prove disruptive or destructive to students? What about faculty? What about the seminary's reputation, and its mission? Could we afford it? Did we have the wherewithal to handle fallout?

In the aftermath of one workshop, I discovered that a resource leader we hired had been showing pornographic films to students in the dorm at night.

Fortunately, I did not have to work in a vacuum dealing with such issues; the dean, members of the faculty, and other administrators weighed in and supported the final decisions. However, I was continuously aware that the community looked to the president for the last word.

Faculty

Having taught at a seminary, I came to Washington understanding the ethos of faculties. It was therefore readily apparent to me that Wesley had an outstanding group—top flight. They were bright, dedicated, and committed to the seminary and the students. They went the extra mile in their endeavors and brought contagious enthusiasm to their work. From day one I felt privileged to serve with them and work in their behalf. I knew they were the beating heart of the seminary. During the difficult financial times before I arrived, they had been the pillar of strength and stability that held everything together. Wesley was blessed to have such a faculty. I had a tremendous appreciation and genuine affection for the faculty as a whole. They made me feel accepted, too.

Every time I had a chance to converse with Wesley graduates, they asked about some particular faculty members, present and past. In every case, they spoke proudly of the positive impact those professors had made on their lives and their ministry. Every time that happened, which was often, I felt encouraged.

I knew from the beginning, however, that although I was listed as a member of the faculty, I was of a different species. I belonged to the administration. I was the president—open to criticism and to inside jokes. I learned very early that however close and friendly I might become with any member of the Wesley community, I was never, ever *not* the president. My wife with some regret in her voice, said, "It used to be fun for us to talk about the administration but now we are it."

The District of Columbia in the 1980s was in turmoil over race, drugs, and violence, with an AIDS pandemic to boot. Wesley was not immune. Tragically, we lost two faculty members and one of our administrative staff to AIDS. I had never encountered such a thing personally or professionally. With some trepidation, I spent private time with each dying member of our community. I led a celebration for their lives and ministry. One of them wanted his ashes buried at Wesley. We honored his request. In his memory we also planted a tree and placed a granite marker beside it.

I sensed that Wesley had retained a certain cultural atmosphere probably brought over from the Westminster days. It was absorbed by even those faculty members who joined after the move. Gradually, normal attrition within our small community paralleled the larger external changes of the turbulent 1980s and brought about a dramatic changing of the guard. By the end of that decade, the faculty makeup had become noticeably different in terms of gender, ethnicity, lifestyle, scholarly preparation, and attitude. More than two-thirds of our new members were either African-American, female, or Hispanic.

I spent considerable time in the hunt for talent. We had at least one major search process underway during each of the 20 years of my tenure. It was enjoyable work, and I have countless memories and stories about it. I learned a lot, not just about the candidates, but about our own faculty. They revealed their ideas and values during the process of quizzing the candidates and pitching what Wesley had to offer.

I stretched myself in many cases to persuade a candidate to join our ranks. Bargaining about salary was not possible since we had a faculty-chosen policy of the same pay at the same rank. We had to settle for accentuating the attractions of our location, our culture, our style of education, and our commitment to the church. On most occasions we succeeded. I can remember only a couple of disappointments.

The Wesley faculty had suffered economically during the seminary's hard times. They fell behind in compensation, benefits, and educational support. The board, with my encouragement, tried to play catch-up in the 1980s, once our budget had been brought into balance. For several years we gave annual raises of 7-8 percent. We beefed up the retirement benefits and made it so that all faculty and (eventually) staff were compensated fairly. We made it possible for faculty and staff with their contributions and the seminary's match to add up to 15 percent of annual salary to their retirement fund.

In addition, we set up a second-mortgage program for faculty and senior administrators to help them afford housing in the expensive Washington area. We revamped the sabbatical policy so as to provide faculty members one full year's sabbatical after six years of teaching. As a means of encouraging younger members in their research and writing, we offered them a one-semester sabbatical after just three years on the job.

IV. Building a Diverse Community

In my inaugural address, two of the goals I proposed for Wesley's future were:

1. Building awareness of globalization—recognizing the growing inter-connectedness of our world and what that

96

meant for a theological school, especially one located in the political capital of the world.

2. Becoming a more diverse seminary—reflecting the diversity of the culture and the constituency we served. We needed to prepare individuals for pastoral leadership, not just by reading and talking about diversity and inclusiveness, but to create an existential community of learning and formation where people had to live, learn, and love people who were different in multiple ways from themselves.

These sounded like lofty goals, even to me, and I was not certain exactly how we could achieve them. I did know that it would take some intentional efforts to become a more diverse and inclusive seminary and to live out that call. There would be no quick-fix solutions. Rather, it would require different strategies over a long period of time. Many factors would contribute to this change process. Some were accidents of history, of location, of theological background, of good fortune, even unintended consequences. Others were intentional actions and planned interventions by a variety of folk. Fundamentally, I believed the seminary had a call to become a more diverse community and a place to live out ministry and prepare others to take it beyond the seminary into the church and the world.

As president I realized I needed to play a pivotal role, even when I was not sure exactly what to do. However, mine was not the only influence. Wesley had already begun its move toward becoming a more diverse and inclusive seminary before I arrived in 1982. In the 1970s the board had rewritten its bylaws to mandate that 20 percent of its members must be racially ethnic. Under the leadership of Dean Phil Wogaman, the school had adopted a language policy with regard to sexuality and had recruited three African-American male faculty members and three female faculty for tenure-track positions.

My intent was to build on those earlier commitments and actions; more was needed. The journey would be longer and more difficult that we imagined. Many groups from the United Methodist Church, the board of governors, the faculty, staff, students, and alumni would need to contribute in essential and timely ways.

Changing the culture of the seminary, or any community, necessitated a long-term process. Commitment and intentional action toward a particular direction would be required, along with a readiness to respond to unexpected opportunities that presented themselves. These responses should be informed and directed by a long-term vision. It demanded patience, persistence, and endurance. There was not one strategy, but the necessity to move on several fronts, always pushing the boundaries. The overall result was that the seminary, through this journey lasting two decades, became a different institution and community. Diversity and inclusiveness became part of Wesley's DNA.

The statistics below show the significant change in the gender and ethnic make-up of the Wesley community from 1982 through 2002:

	1982	2002
Students	12% Ethnic of 350	40% Ethnic of 700
Faculty	14% Ethnic of 22	23% Ethnic of 26
	14% Female of 22	42% Female of 26
Staff	15% Ethnic	30% Ethnic
Senior Admin	1 Ethnic Male	2 Ethnic Females
	4 Caucasian Males	1 Caucasian Female
Board of Gov.	20% Ethnic	29% Ethnic
	20% Female	26% Female

Assumptions Behind Our Commitment to Diversity

- Theologically, we believed we were all parts of the body of Christ and needed each other to become what God intended for us.
- We lived in an increasingly interconnected world and, as author Tom Friedman reminded us, an increasingly flat world.
- To prepare leaders to function effectively in this world, they must be educated and formed not just by reading or talking about diversity, but they must existentially live and learn in such a community.
- Ethnicity and gender held prominent positions in Wesley's concept of a diverse community. Wesley also recognized that a diverse community could include persons from different theological perspectives, denominational backgrounds, sexual preferences, socio-economic status, and geographical origins.

Wesley Seminary's Geographic, Ethnographic, and Strategic Advantage

Wesley had a number of geographic, ethnographic, and strategic advantages for becoming a more diverse seminary. First, its location in the nation's capital made it a national and global attraction. Through a strong migration in the 1950s and 60s of African Americans seeking jobs in the government and related industries, Washington increased the African-American population to a 65 percent majority with many strong African-American churches. Methodism in American and later African-American Methodist groups—AME, CME, and AME Zion—all originated in the mid-Atlantic region and retained strong churches in that region. The Washington Episcopal Area of the United Methodist Church had the second largest number of African-American churches of any Episcopal area after South Carolina.

Finally, the Washington region had a rapidly-growing population, almost a 2 million increase in 20 years. That population also had the highest percentage of college graduates—people eligible for graduate education—of any section of the country.

All of these factors provided advantages for Wesley in terms of attracting racially diverse individuals to the seminary. They did not, however, guarantee that the seminary would become a more diverse institution. It meant that the potential was there should the seminary embark on a strategic effort to become more inclusive and diverse.

In the Beginning

An opportunity presented itself early in my tenure. The Commission on Religion and Race of the United Methodist Church was urging all United Methodist institutions to conduct racism workshops on their home turf. Since the Commission was located in Washington, early in my second year I suggested to the Wesley board, faculty, and staff that we might participate as one of the pilot groups. Everyone agreed. The staff of the Commission came to campus and led an eight-hour workshop designed to educate us on the nature of racism, how it was present in our midst, and challenging us to decide how we were going to change ourselves individually and our seminary as a community.

Near the end of the workshop Roy Morrison, the longest serving African-American faculty member, stood up and addressed the assembled group of board, faculty, and staff. Roy, an extremely bright and articulate philosophical theologian with a University of Chicago

Ph.D., but with a deep reservoir of anger, unleashed a 10-minute tirade about the racism at Wesley seminary and its racist president. "All of this liberal talk," he asserted, "covered over with a gentile veneer doesn't mean shit." Roy had a vast vocabulary of expletives that he could fully display in such moments, and he used most of them on that occasion.

His angry words traumatized the gathered assembly. I looked directly at Roy the whole time he was speaking, but I said nothing in response. A long silence followed. Then Wayne Smithey, the chair of the Wesley board of governors, stood up and said to Roy: "Dr. Morrison, we are grateful for you reminding us of the deep wounds among us and how in this community we have acted out of our racism both knowingly and unknowingly in our history. I want you to know that the board of governors and I will do everything in our power to eradicate these stains of racism and to build a new Wesley community that will prepare a new generation of leaders who can lead our churches and our communities to remove the invasive blot of racism in our society. Furthermore, I am tonight appointing Isham Baker to chair a new affirmative action committee, made up of four members of the board along with faculty and student representatives to develop an affirmative action program that can lead us in this effort." Isham Baker, an African American, an architect, an active churchman, was one of the most respected members of the board. The committee consisted of two African Americans, one male and one female, and one white male and a white female. Smithey served ex-officio on the committee.

A palpable sigh of relief spread throughout the group. Finally, Smithey said, "This has been a very important occasion in the life of Wesley Seminary. We have learned much and know we have much to do. We have done

101

enough for the moment. I am going to call on our president to dismiss us with a prayer." I honestly cannot remember what I said. What I do know is that Wayne Smithey exercised the essence of good leadership at that moment and rendered a gift of God's grace to those gathered members of the Wesley Seminary community.

A few weeks later I took Roy and the two other African-American faculty members to lunch. I wanted to hear how they perceived African-Americans at Wesley and what suggestions they had for me as president. Roy spoke with more restraint on that occasion, but he still used colorful language to assail me and the seminary for our slowness in making changes in racist attitudes and structural barriers that weighed on African-Americans in the seminary.

After Roy died a few years later, these other two faculty members and I were reflecting on Roy and his contributions to Wesley. One of them, remembering that first racism workshop, said, "We could not have done what Roy did. But his anger and forcefulness did break a logjam at Wesley Seminary and set us on a new path. Furthermore, your listening to Roy's wrath without blaming or retreating, your reaching out and hanging in, helped set a new tone and direction for all of us."

They did not know my personal journey with Roy. Three or four years after the "blow up," Roy and I met by chance in London's Heathrow airport. He had spent a week at Trinity College, Cambridge, as a guest lecturer in philosophical theology. It was the pinnacle of his professional career. We sat together on the seven-hour flight across the Atlantic and discussed philosophical theology. Roy was writing his magnum opus, a long and complicated book—*Science, Theology, and the Transcendental Horizon: Einstein, Kant, and Tillich.* He later gave me a copy of the manuscript, which I plowed through the next summer and sent him several comments and questions. Roy could not believe that I understood what he was talking about and that I invested time and interest in him. From that point forward Roy became one of my arch supporters and advocates on the faculty. I learned a lot from Roy, not just about philosophical theology, but about the pains of racism and what it was like to grow up and live in our society as an African-American male. He was a gift of grace to me and the Wesley community in many, often hidden, ways.

Affirmative Action Policy and Goals

Isham Baker provided outstanding leadership to our affirmative action committee. Over the next two years the committee drafted an affirmative action policy and a set of goals for the seminary. These were vetted with the faculty, administration, staff, students, and finally passed by the board. Some of the most important goals and policies were:

1. The ethnic make-up of the seminary staff will reflect the ethnic make-up of the Washington region.
2. The ethnic make-up of the student body will reflect the ethnic make-up of the United Methodist Church and the churches Wesley serves in its region.
3. The make-up of the faculty will reflect the ethnic and gender make-up of the student body.
4. At least 20 percent of the board of governors will be racially diverse.
5. Wesley Seminary will have an affirmative action officer who will be nominated by the president, affirmed by the board, and will report to the board of governors. The AAO will report to the

board on the make-up of the Wesley student body, the staff, faculty, and administration, including all hiring processes and results for the year.

6. There will be an affirmative action committee of five people with at least one representative from each of the following—faculty, staff, administration, board, and student body. The committee will work with the Affirmative Action Officer to: 1) receive complaints regarding racial or gender issues from the community; 2) where necessary refer these issues to the administration or to the board through the AAO; 3) receive reports from the AAO concerning hiring processes and other issues in the seminary; 4) recommend and encourage educational programs in the seminary designed to address racial and gender issues.

7. In all seminary searches every effort will be made to include females and persons of color among the candidates.

8. The affirmative action officer will be informed about and monitor all search processes conducted by the seminary.

During the 1980s the committee and the AAO helped to set the tone and drive the seminary's efforts toward diversity and inclusiveness. They also acted as a burr under the saddle of the president and dean, particularly around hiring processes. I worked diligently in the search and recruitment of ethnic faculty as called for in the affirmative action plan. We made a special and successful effort to recruit Josiah Young, a young African-American theologian from Colgate University. A faculty report to the board recognized this effort: "This youthful, black, two-career family would likely not have come had the president not extended himself and the resources of the seminary to resolve several problems that figured into their decision."

The Association of Black Seminarians

In the 1980s the seminary had an active association of black seminarians led by a group of aggressive students who pushed racism issues and were often confrontational with the administration. Once in a meeting with the president and dean, they pushed hard on some issues. I supported the students because they were right on the issues they were pushing. That confrontation created some stress within the administration, but it built trust with the African-American students. They no longer felt the administration would merely stonewall their issues and automatically disregard their ideas and perspectives. The Association also did a good job of keeping in touch with African-American graduates of Wesley and encouraged their involvement with the students and in the life of the seminary.

Role of the Board of Governors

Since the mid-1970s, Wesley's board of governors had an abiding commitment to diversity and inclusiveness. They had changed the bylaws mandating that 20 percent of the board be African-American. In the 1980s they strongly supported the affirmative action policies and program and were encouraging of every initiative the administration proposed to enhance or advance the seminary's efforts toward diversity. Later in the affirmative action goals, they strongly urged that we seek and hire an African-American female for the faculty. Many of the members forcefully spoke to the president: "Do what it takes to bring an African-American female to the faculty."

Following Wayne Smithey's four-year tenure, Helen Smith became chair of the board. She was very effective and provided high visibility as a woman in a key leadership position in the seminary. Isham Baker, the first African-American chair of the board, followed her. He was well known in the Washington area and among African-American churches and their pastors. He brought a tremendous presence and symbol for Wesley. He spent countless hours representing the seminary in strategic occasions on and off the campus. Wesley later named another African American as chair of the board.

A number of other African-American members of the board, both clergy and laity, were helpful in connecting and advocating for Wesley among African-American churches and denominations in the Washington region. Without a doubt their presence on the board and their advocacy for the seminary encouraged a number of African-American students to attend Wesley. One African-American Baptist pastor, who ultimately joined the board, sent more students to Wesley than any five churches combined—regardless of ethnic makeup.

Important Strategic Initiatives

During this two-decade move toward increased diversity, Wesley Seminary and its leadership were clear in their strategies and initiatives. Some actions were planned over an extended period. Others were opportunities, almost serendipitous moments, that presented themselves. But each required some action and commitment to a particular program or intervention into the community's life and structures. Some posed significant risks. A few I called wedge-opportunities that required driving an initiative through a small opening that expanded as it grew and begin to affect the larger seminary community. In some cases these initiatives were not widely supported in the beginning, but support grew with their successes. Almost every initiative engendered some opposition or resistance from some quarter of the seminary.

The following are some of the more significant and pivotal initiatives that helped to reshape Wesley Seminary.

1. In my first year as president, when Phil Wogaman stepped down as dean, I insisted, in the face of resistance from some members of the faculty, that we conduct a national search. That search secured Marjorie Suchochi from Pittsburgh Theological School as the dean. She was not only the first female dean at Wesley, but was the first female dean of any United Methodist seminary.

2. Following that explosive first racism workshop, a group of students insisted on sponsoring a racism workshop for students. The retreat was so successful that a planning committee of faculty and students recommended that the seminary hold a social issues retreat annually. Each retreat had a Friday-through-Saturday timetable, a wide variety of educational experiences, and a focus on one major social issue such as racism, sexism, human sexuality, drugs and alcohol, etc. All students would be required to participate in two such retreats during their degree programs at Wesley and all faculty and administrative staff were expected to participate. After considerable debate and resistance from all quarters, the program was launched.

The retreats were dynamite, both positively and negatively. They exposed all of us to ideas, prejudices, and feelings of others as well as our own, They exposed and confronted us with other types of individuals, their hopes and dreams, that we may never have experienced otherwise. They also stirred up deep feelings, anger, fears, and unfulfilled expectations that all of us were harboring. The seminary, unfortunately, had no adequate means of processing all the material that was uncovered. The movement nevertheless lasted six years until it was quietly laid to rest after we were too exhausted to protest. Those issues retreats, however, did keep the community aware of how deep and difficult were the barriers, the fears, and the prejudices we were grappling with while trying to become a more diverse community that we felt called to become.

3. A third initiative concerned globalization. During my first few years at Wesley, we promoted a consciousness about globalization. For two years we invited a visiting professor from South Africa. We began a cooperative DMin with the United Methodist seminaries in Europe. We hosted a group of 18 Russian Orthodox students for two days on our campus, and they led us in Orthodox worship in our chapel. We even experimented with an educational travel program run by two individuals from Shenandoah College. Many members of our faculty, staff, and student body participated in demonstrations at the South African embassy against apartheid. I served as the chair of the Association of United Methodist Theological School's committee on globalization. All of these efforts kept concerns about the issues of globalization alive at Wesley, but none of them had significant impact on the seminary or its programs.

A big opportunity emerged through Plowshares Institute, which received a large grant to work on the globalization of theological education. It involved 12 seminaries from across ATS. During the four-year life of the project, representative groups from the faculty, administration, and board of each school participated in three international immersions and then designed a local immersion of its own. Each seminary had a local steering committee, which helped each immersion group prepare and debrief. In addition, it would lead the school in planning and acting on what it had learned and the implications for the seminary's education programs. Since I chaired the Plowshares Board, I made sure Wesley was one of the chosen seminaries. At the same time we participated in a Palestine Awareness program that took a large number of Wesley's faculty, administration, and board for 10-day immersion to Palestine.

During the project almost all the faculty of Wesley, all the senior administrators, and several of the members of the board participated in various immersions to China, South Africa, India, Eastern Europe, and South America. Wesley's own local immersion was to take the whole faculty and some board members on a four-day immersion in Appalachia and then four-day in the inner-city of Washington. We confronted amazing experiences from snake-handling churches in West Virginia to the poverty of the inner-city of Washington. We all ended up sleeping in the basement of a church like a high school youth group. The amazing thing is that we all came out of the overall experience still speaking to each other.

As it turned out, these globalization experiences picked up where the issues retreats left off, emotionally and educationally. They continued to heighten our consciousness and pushed us to refocus how we were educating and forming people for ministry. Out of them came the awareness of how unconnected we were both in knowledge and commitment to the global scene and to our local communities and cultures out of which our students came and in which they would serve in ministry. It is hard to document all that emerged from that four-year journey. I do know that the Wesley faculty began to teach differently, their syllabi included new materials, and many now required implementation projects from their course material. The faculty introduced a new curriculum requirement that all masters-degree candidates must earn credit for an immersion experience into a culture different from their own. I had proposed, encouraged, and participated in all of these experiences. Through them my colleagues and I got to know each other better. I also learned more about myself. The experiences heightened my sensitivity to diversity and inclusiveness issues at Wesley, in our world and local community.

4. We all were aware that Wesley had very little Hispanic and Asian presence among the students, staff, or faculty and we wanted to improve that. The dean and I made an intense effort to recruit our first Hispanic faculty member into a position we had to create. Our efforts at Hispanic student recruitment despite the best seminary's efforts did not bear much fruit.

 On the Asian front we were presented with another serendipitous gift. In 1991 Wesley had two Asian students—a Korean in the MDiv program and a Korean female in the DMin program. We had an opening for a part-time dean of students. Someone suggested the Korean female in the DMin I interviewed Kyunglim Shin Lee, perceived terrific potential in her, and hired her without a competitive search. She turned out to be a dynamo. What happened in the next 10 years again helped to transform Wesley. We went from one to 35 Korean MDiv students, plus two Korean DMin groups. We developed a supportive network of Korean churches, pastors, and laity in Korea and the U.S. that fed us students and contributed to a Korean scholarship fund now nearly $3 million. Kyunglim arranged and led a number of immersions to Korea for students, faculty, and some board members. During this period Wesley added a

Korean faculty member and three members to the board. Finally, Kwanglim Church, located in Seoul, Korea, and the largest Methodist congregation in the world (85,000 members) endowed a chair in world missions in their pastor's name. He was Sundo Kim, Wesley's first Korean graduate.

My role in this explosive development was to encourage, support, and protect our Korean dean from some resentful members of the Wesley community whose feathers she sometimes ruffled. I spoke at many Korean gatherings and made seven trips to Korea to preach, teach, and build relationships. I even developed an eight-word Korean vocabulary and grew to love the Korean people, their food, and culture. This dean now serves as vice president for international relations at Wesley.

This globalization initiative eventually fostered another significant step on our road to diversity and inclusiveness. Wesley called a theologian from India to occupy the new chair in world missions, endowed by Kwanglim Church. This call helped the seminary community continue its multicultural journey and interfaith dialogue.

5. During the mid-1980s Wesley struggled with how to recruit more African-American students. Two clear factors emerged—finances and course availability.

First, we recognized that most African-American students who considered coming to Wesley Seminary had fewer financial resources than their white counterparts. We had to address financial aid. Because of its serious budgetary difficulties Wesley only offered financial aid to full-time students, and only in their first year of study. The seminary hoped that once students matriculated, they would remain and finish the degree without further assistance. We altered that strategy by taking dramatic and risky steps:

1. To get more money into the financial-aid budget, we increased tuition one year by 23 percent and put 15 percent into financial aid and allocated additional funds from the regular budget
2. Part-time students would be eligible for financial aid
3. Any aid package given would now be available for three years so each student would know what to count on throughout his/her degree program
4. All students were eligible for financial aid, not just United Methodist students
5. All racial ethnic students would automatically receive an additional 20 percent on their financial aid grant
6. A Wesley Scholar program was established. One scholarship would be given annually to an outstanding African-American student. It would cover full tuition plus a stipend for three years of full-time study

A few board members wondered whether we should give so much aid to non-United Methodist students. A few students questioned the 20 percent add-on for racial ethnic students, but in general everyone was pleased and excited about this new financial aid program because it reached many more students. An immediate bump in African-American student applications occurred along with additional applications from white students as well.

More important for African-American students we began to offer degree credit courses in the evening, including some of the required courses. Initially, a majority of the faculty resisted, many saying they could not and would not teach evening courses. They insisted that persons should never be allowed to take all of their courses in the evening. Gradually the faculty began to understand the missional goals involved in this direction and became willing to teach evening courses. Some even taught in experimental Saturday courses. By the 1990s Wesley was offering all of its required courses in the evening as well as during the day. It became possible to earn a degree by taking mostly night courses.

These two initiatives in effect opened the floodgates for African-American students at Wesley. Many working persons, male and female, black and white, began to perceive the seminary as a desirable and now financially viable option. Wesley became widely regarded as a cutting-edge seminary committed to diversity and inclusiveness that offered a quality education in an ecumenical and integrated setting.

African-American women in particular, whose denominations and culture discouraged females in ministry, found affirmation and opportunity at Wesley. Many also discovered in the United Methodist Church opportunities for ordained ministry. As their denominations and churches began to open up opportunities for women, they shared their stories with their churches and communities and made converts of their pastors and congregations. Plus, the seminary's African-American faculty members were highly respected and actively engaged evangelists for Wesley Seminary. The result was a multiplier effect for Wesley to attract more and more African-American students. By 2000 Wesley enrolled more than 200 African-American students.^

6. The most difficult and frustrating initiative was Wesley's effort to recruit an African-American female to the faculty. During the 1980s several African-American

females were in the candidate pools in searches. In one case the finalist was an African-American woman. After much discussion and debate, we decided not to call her. The community's response was immediately irate. The black graduates association was upset. The board urged us to do better and find an acceptable African-American woman for the faculty. Some felt we should hire any qualified African-American woman regardless of her academic field, whether we needed an additional faculty person in that field or not. African-American women as adjuncts—we had two or three—would not do. They must be in a tenure-track position.

A year later, after much searching and behind the scenes work by the dean and president, we located a highly recommended young African-American woman in a field where we had a vacancy, but who was only halfway through her Ph.D. program. With faculty support and board approval we entered into an agreement with her. She would finishes her prelim exams the next year and then teach half time at Wesley and work on her dissertation while on full salary. We even found a job for her husband at American University. This three-year effort, however, ended sadly and disappointingly. Her husband took a job at another university and never came to Washington. She, after two years of commuting and part-time teaching, decided not to finish her doctoral program. She left to go into parish ministry and cut her ties with Wesley.

Disappointed and almost in despair, the faculty voted not to fill another faculty position unless it was with an African-American female. Frankly, as we conducted our next two or three searches, the school probably bordered on acting illegally according to the current employment law. Finally, we were able to fill a vacancy on the faculty with an African-American woman who was a Wesley grad. She was writing her dissertation. We assisted her and lightened her teaching load until she completed the degree. Within a couple of years the seminary was able to hire another tenure track African-American female.

Personal Learning

This "journey to diversity" taught me many lessons about the role of leadership. Paramount among them is how important it is for the leader to name the issues, to hold up a vision, and to set goals.

The leader—the president—must invest considerable time and energy to create a protective umbrella for the project and for the participating individuals. This may at times call for bold action. Sometimes risk may be involved, as when we hired the first female academic dean and the first Asian dean of community life.

We went further by pushing for initiatives such as the first racism workshop, the issues retreat program, the globalization program, the first Korean dean, and the first African-American woman added to the faculty. We hired African-American women in the positions of administrative assistant and executive secretary, and they both had a positive influence within the Wesley community and outside as well.

On the flip side, there is hardly any doubt that we represented a threat to some in the majority community and created resentment in the areas of financial aid, faculty searches, board membership, and the like. Was our progress worth that cost? I think so.

I lived in hope that the movement toward inclusiveness in our society in that last half of the 20th century would move beyond diversity to becoming a multicultural and interfaith society that cuts across racial, religious, social, economic, and political lines. This evolution still feels like a dream and will require some new language, new types of communities, new faith assumptions and perspectives, and some new leadership. Our theological schools need to be in the forefront of this new society, helping us understand its faith roots, the resulting life changes needed, the social reordering, and how we call, prepare, and sustain religious leadership for this new day.

Appreciation

I want to acknowledge my gratitude to all members of the Wesley community who are unnamed in this story. In multiple and courageous ways they contributed to transforming Wesley Seminary into a more diverse and inclusive community of God's people. We shared our lives, our fears, our frustrations, our hopes, and dreams together for 20 years and in turn changed ourselves and Wesley Seminary.

V. Enrollment

Enrollment tells a critical story about the health and vitality of an institution. Everyone wants to know what the numbers are. Faculty members want assurance that their classrooms will be full. Board members wonder if the school is fulfilling its mission. Students want to know how many others have made the same choice they did. The staff wonders what their workload will be. The president worries about tuition income and tracks the numbers assiduously.

Wesley's enrollment in the 1980s posed some compelling questions and challenges. The following statistics give a snapshot of enrollment during those years.

Year	MDiv	MRE/MA	MTS	DMin	Others	Total	Tuition Hrs
1981-82	223	11	20	37	36	327	6228
1982-83	224	14	24	39	38	339	6300
1983-84	267	17	29	33	30	376	7578
1984-85	280	22	35	30	25	392	7682
1985-86	263	19	30	28	30	370	6770
1986-87	240	15	39	38	28	360	6408
1987-88	235	22	34	36	32	359	6436
1988-89	230	15	42	41	35	363	6383
1989-90	231	16	43	54	48	392	6496
1990-91	237	17	44	68	41	407	6740

By the 1980s, most colleges and universities had become effective in recruiting students. Although seminaries also had become more sophisticated in their recruiting efforts, they still lagged far behind. Wesley was no exception. Annually we would pore over the enrollment figures trying to decide if we were in the midst of a trend we could not control or we were not doing a good-enough job enlisting students. Usually it was a bit of both.

Recruitment/Admissions

Change took place gradually in the seminary world, largely driven by economics. Traditionally the primary concept was "admissions"—how do we screen applicants to make sure we are admitting quality students who have potential for ministerial leadership. The admission gate opened through a committee consisting mostly of faculty. They read the applications and decided who should be allowed through the door. In the 1980s, that responsibility shifted to the admissions office. Faculty continued to advise with regard to standards, but did not retain veto power. The administration, noting what the colleges were doing, began to look at the ratio of inquiries to the number of applications to the number of applicants who were admitted.

During the first few years of my tenure, I had to navigate a learning curve with regard to enrollment. As I gradually made the connection between enrollment and budget, I became more attentive to how well we performed in the admissions process. Were we producing the enrollment we required? Along the way, I also discovered that retention had a significant impact on overall enrollment.

Enrollment Decline

During my second year (1983-84), Wesley experienced a sharp uptick in the number of enrollments. That continued for three years and made it easier to balance the budget. I thought we must be doing something right, and I found it rather enjoyable to be considered something of an economic genius. A precipitous downturn then made it clear that I had just been lucky. From 1986 to 1990 we had 30 to 40 fewer MDiv students, which resulted in a total loss of some $120 thousand per year. Balancing the budget became trickier.

In 1988 I shared an ATS report with the board showing that we were not alone; MDiv enrollment was declining in theological schools across the country. To make up for these losses, schools were developing other degree programs at the Masters and DMin levels. We got the message and began to ramp up our recruitment efforts and put more resources into degree programs other than the MDiv.

A second trend of the 1980s began to emerge: the complexion of our student body was changing markedly. No longer did we see a preponderance of young white males on the campus. We saw many students in their 40s; we saw women; we saw ethnic diversity; we saw part-time students become the majority. The latter change was the primary cause of a reduction in the average annual course load of a student. From 1980 through 1988 the annual hours per student dropped from 22.7 tuition hours to 18. By 1990, the average load had fallen to 16.6.

Enrollment and the Budget

In light of another evolving trend, that decline had ominous implications—the seminary's dependence on tuition income was increasing steadily. During the 1980s, the percentage of income from tuition rose from 30 to 37 percent. By the year 2000, it would become more than 45 percent. Wesley was not unusual in that regard. Except for those few schools with large endowments, most seminaries became increasingly tuition-dependent.

The message was clear. We needed to roll up our sleeves and do a better job of recruiting—which we did. By 1992 we had more than 300 students on the MDiv track for the first time ever. Even so, we were swimming against a strong tide; it took that number of MDiv students to equal the income from just 225 in the early 1980s. In order to increase the tuition hours, we had to increase enrollment in areas besides MDiv, notably the MTS and DMin programs.

Simple figures show a clear connection between enrollment and budget. The cost of tuition was $95 an hour in 1982. We had to raise that by just a little over 5 percent in 1983, which seemed modest at the time. Circumstances gave us little choice but to continue a similar percentage of increase annually, plus a special one-time increase in 1987. By the year 2000, the cost per tuition-hour had risen to a shocking $345. That increase of 263 percent was three times the rise in the Consumer Price Index across that span of time.

119

Financial Aid

From day one I had an ever-present concern about financial assistance for students. The seminary awarded scholarships only to first-year students. The assumption was that once they got started, they would find a way to fund the other years, but that was not always the case. We finally made a big change in 1986-87. To build up the scholarship pool, we increased tuition by 23%, from $132 per hour to $162. The additional income we put in the scholarship pool. That allowed us to make scholarship assistance available for three years for qualifying students, even those who were part-time.

Student Loans

The real game-changer for student funding was the federal government's guaranteed student loan program. At the outset, seminary students could borrow up to $5,000 a year with no interest until they finished school. The limit continued to rise, along with the amount of paperwork. Navigating all the governmental regulations attached to those loans increased our administrative time and cost. We shifted the burden onto the shoulders of our new dean of students, Linda Thomas. She in turn had to take on extra help. Despite having no previous experience in that area, she did a thorough and effective job.

Wesley also qualified for a new federal work study program which paid students for numerous jobs in the seminary. Management of that program also became attached to the dean of student's office. The new work-demands quickly became overwhelming. Linda spent a large portion of her time administering financial aid. Insufficient time remained for the traditional duties of a dean. Ultimately, the student council issued a protest and called for a change. We responded by moving the first-year scholarship awards to the admission office, where they could be integrated into the recruiting program. Eventually, we had to appoint a full-time director of financial aid.

Before long, educational institutions in all 50 states found their budgets stretched to the breaking point. There were three primary causes: the need to offer better service to their students, the requirement to comply with new government regulations, and the need to keep pace with technological advancements.

Linda's experience working directly with students who were taking out guaranteed student loans led her to raise serious concerns about the amount of debt students would carry into their pastoral ministries. She alerted all of us to the looming financial problem for future pastors and their churches. We did our best to heed her prophetic warnings. We set up personal budget management seminars for students who applied for loans. We also tried to develop a policy that would limit how much a student could borrow, but that did not work. One student reminded us that he had a legal right to borrow that money, and we had no legal right to stand in his way. Our concerns remained, but the cycle of rising expenses, increasingly funded by tuition and, often as not, paid by student loans, continued without letup. Today, many educators as well as business and government officials point to an upcoming crisis. The current level of student-loan debt in the United States stands at more than a trillion dollars.

One final example shows the complexity of the loan issue with regard to Wesley. The seminary had a policy that students could not register for the next semester's classes if they had an unpaid balance in their accounts. That brought up a classic Catch-22 situation: some students could not pay their bills until they received their next loan, but they could not receive the loan until they had enrolled.

The seminary amassed a sizable shortfall from unpaid tuition and fees. Some students withdrew from school owing money. Others stood ready to graduate, but we could not issue a diploma until their accounts were clear. In many cases the seminary had no choice but to write off a certain amount of debt.

Many emotional crises were attached to this unfortunate situation, and more than a few of them fell into my lap. Worthy individuals who would be valued members of the clergy begged for rescue, whether by extension of their unpaid bill or by scholarship aid. Caught in a vise between their needs and the needs of the seminary, I faced some of my most excruciating decisions.

VI. Change in Senior Administrative Team

In my first year I was confronted with the need to fill three of the four senior administrative positions—dean, development, and business office. I was very fortunate. This reconstructed senior management team was talented and worked extremely well together for two years. The vice president for development was then called to become president of Saint Paul School of Theology. The dean of students, who was teaching half-time, wanted to move to a full-time teaching position. I supported his move.

I was pleased for Lovett Weems' opportunity to become a seminary president. He was extraordinarily talented and hard-working, possessing leadership qualities that would fit him well for a presidency. His leaving, however, created a huge hole in the seminary's development office. We had made significant progress, annually increasing our fundraising capacity and beginning to think about our first capital campaign.

I was in a dilemma. David McAllister-Wilson was still a student in the MDiv program. He had become an important part of the seminary's development team, but he had no experience managing a development office and program. After talking with our development consultant and members of the board of governors, I launched a search for a new vice president for development. Surprisingly, an attractive candidate quickly emerged. He came strongly recommended. He had a warm and engaging personality and expressed strong interest in the job. I moved quickly and offered him the job.

Within a few months, however, he and I recognized that fundraising was not his cup of tea. We explored an alternative arrangement but he submitted a gracious letter of resignation saying he thought his talents could be better used in a different job.

I felt remorse, knowing that I had made a mistake in the selection process. An individual's performance in a job is his/her responsibility. But, it is also a failure on the leader's part for inadequate judgment in placing the person in that position in the first place and for not adequately supervising, supporting, and training that person to do the job. I also bore responsibility.

I also learned that once I realized that the match of job and person would not work, I had the responsibility to make a change. Churches and seminaries too often delay action on job/person misfits or refuse to remove someone because they do not want to hurt or mistreat the individual. Removal is hard but allowing a person who is inadequately performing in a crucial institutional job can penalize everyone. If the seminary suffers in one area from poor personnel performance, everyone connected to the seminary suffers to some degree, even when they cannot always see the connection. The leader has ultimate responsibility to connect those dots and not allow the institution and its mission to be damaged inappropriately. Nevertheless, I always viewed personnel changes as difficult and painful.

Complications

The development office position became more complicated. Lovett Weems was working diligently to turn around Saint Paul seminary. He wanted David McAllister-Wilson to serve as his vice president for development. It was a tempting offer. Lovett and David had become close friends and effective colleagues.

David was a talented young man with great potential. Losing another key person in the development office at that moment would have been a disastrous blow to our fundraising efforts, which were just beginning to bloom. I was deeply conflicted. Should I elevate him to vice president so quickly and without his having any experience in managing a program and staff? He had great potential but needed the opportunity to grow. Becoming a VP was clearly in his future if he could prove himself as a manager, finish his degree, and mature as a valued senior administrator at Wesley. I asked him to assume responsibility for managing the development program, but with the title of director of development.

I affirmed David in every way possible and assured him of my confidence in him and his future. This latest move would also make him a member of the administrative council.

I held my breath for a few weeks until David decided to remain at Wesley. In the coming years he would become my most trusted and important colleague in leading Wesley Seminary.

Dean of Students

The search for a new dean of students took almost a year because I wanted an ethnic woman who had the right talent and would bring to the position experience in and commitment to ministry. We finally landed Linda Thomas, an African-American woman. She had been a United Methodist pastor but was looking for a position with a different challenge and an opportunity to grow. She found that at Wesley Seminary. She in turn became an important and valued member of the administration for five years.

For the next three years the Administrative Council became one of the most creative and effective senior leadership teams in my two decades at Wesley.

Other Personnel Changes

When I came to Wesley, Jean Murphy was the president's secretary. She continued in that position for six more years, which was lucky for me. She was gracious, efficient, and indispensable during that critical time when I was learning the ropes.

When Jean retired I hired Joyce Emmerling as secretary and expanded the office to include Cora Pinkney as executive assistant to the president. She managed the overall administration of the office and focused on supporting our work with the board of governors and personnel policies for the seminary. Cora, an African-American woman, was quiet and reserved but enormously helpful to me in working with the African-

American community at Wesley and in the Washington area African-American churches.

Personnel Searches

We were always in the hunt for new people, whether faculty, administrators, board members, or staff. I knew that who was on the Wesley bus and which seats they occupied was critical to the seminary's effectiveness and well-being. I thus committed a significant portion of my time to personnel hunts of various sorts. In the end it felt like the "right" investment. Gradually I discovered that I had my own set of personnel criteria and questions. I looked for ambitious people who set goals and pursued them with drive and energy. I wanted individuals with ambition, who could help us effect changes in the system. I put a premium on creativity and hoped the candidates would bring diversity to the seminary and would fit in with our culture. I also confess that I looked for people I liked and felt I could trust.

VII. Building the Board of Governors

A Problem

Whatever attributes its members possessed as individuals, Wesley's board of governors had never studied its collective image in a mirror. It had never participated in a careful assessment of itself nor formulated a plan for its own continuing evaluation, development, and education. Even as Wesley drifted to the very threshold of bankruptcy in the early 1980s, the board appeared unable to help right the foundering ship. The further concept of guiding it toward a bright future seemed out of reach. There would be no quick-and-easy fix for that, but something had to be done. I therefore made it one of my top priorities to transform the board of governors into an instrument of strength before the decade came to an end.

The Road to Recovery

Our early efforts produced a new means of selecting board members and board leaders. A small grant from Lilly Endowment in 1984 provided additional momentum. It was a one-year grant specifically for developing an education plan for board members. We presented that plan to Lilly Endowment staff with a stated goal of "preparing members to serve to their maximum potential." We started with the assessment of the strengths and abilities of each member, including background and special interests. This was followed with a program of demonstrating how the seminary and the board could team up in drafting the blueprint for a bright future.

When that grant expired, the Endowment offered a second-stage, three-year proposal focused on board development. It was larger in size as well in length. Wesley would receive $20,000 each year and match it with $10,000. As part of the announcement, Lilly Endowment's vice president for religion, Robert Lynn, conducted a workshop for the board. He presented each member with a copy of Robert Greenleaf's book, *Seminary as Servant*. Then at the annual Wesley Council banquet, he spoke about the need for good stewards to govern our precious theological schools, and the importance of a seminary's role in the church and society.

With these grants for leverage, we put renewed vigor into the search for talent. Our board members were elected for one four-year term and could be re-elected twice. Traditionally, a new member would begin those 12 years serving on a committee, followed by committee

127

chairmanship. In due course, he or she might become an officer of the board. Then, with a seeming abruptness that often astonished me, a member's term would expire. The task of recruiting and evaluating new candidates was thus never-ending.

Cultivating prospects was interesting and stimulating, but not the first priority. The grant helped us first build a framework to support the elements of a quality search. We engaged ourselves more fully than ever before in defining the characteristics of a suitable candidate and setting standards for evaluation and selection. We devised a chart to guide the assessment process. It contained five major criteria:

1. Commitment to the Church—active in local church, denomination, or ecumenical organizations
2. Willingness to Invest Time—participation in board meetings, committees, special assignments
3. Expertise—organizational, interpersonal, and special skills
4. Influence—influence in the church and society, use of influence for Wesley, and ability to recruit others in the service of the seminary
5. Financial support—potential for annual and capital support

Having developed the criteria for new members, we decided to use them to evaluate current board members as well. Working on the instrument awakened the committee and then the whole board to the critical role and the enormous potential the board possessed to spearhead the growth and development of the seminary. It put a charge of excitement into the recruiting effort. It would prove to be a watershed along a path toward transforming the board that I had envisioned. The investment of time and energy was well spent.

Recruitment

Recommendations for board candidates came from various sources. A Wesley alumnus might suggest someone from his or her congregation. Current board members offered suggestions, as did some members of the faculty. I kept my eyes peeled, too. One thing became standard: when a prospect showed up on our radar, I scheduled a face-to-face meeting with that person. That afforded me the chance to share facts about the seminary and its mission, about our students and our faculty, and the leadership role of the board. It also allowed me to judge the candidate's potential and decide whether to take the next step—an invitation. I always went into those initial meetings with some knowledge of the individual based on what the recommender had told me.

Sometimes it was love at first sight, and at other times there was a period of courtship. Strange as it might seem, once offered our invitations were rarely turned down. It was not just the result of my persuasive power. The recommended candidates would have deep values and commitment to the church and its future leadership. A willingness to talk to a seminary president already provided a positive signal of interest on their part. Each one had a different story and a different interest that brought him or her to our doorstep. One woman said, "I am doing this for my grandchildren. I want them to have a good and influential church in their lives." Another candidate said he was interested only if his wife could be involved in some way. He did say yes, she did get involved, and they became valuable assets to the seminary.

After each meeting, I took my recommendation to the board's development committee. Together we surveyed our prospects to match the board's openings, present and future. If we had no immediate vacancy for a qualified candidate, I would often invite him or her to join the president's advisory council as a way of serving the seminary while waiting in the wings.

Personal Notes

My role with the board extended beyond recruiting new members. Quite often I asked current board members for various commitments—to serve in a leadership role, give financial support, help with recruiting, and so forth. Such occasions were often memorable. They put me in close touch with individuals and allowed me to appreciate their unique gifts and personalities. A notable example was Martha Carr. She inevitably expressed her feelings of inadequacy for any task requested of her. I once asked her to co-chair a major campaign. She gave the standard answer—she could not possibly do that. The next Sunday in church she was sitting in the pew ahead of Shirley and me. In his sermon the pastor made a strong point that we are often summoned, as Christians, to say yes to God's call. I passed her a note: "Just say yes!" She returned a note: "I presume this means you also want a large gift from me." My return note contained one word: "Yes!" She did ultimately say yes to being co-chair and to making a very significant financial gift to the campaign. She retained her shy and self-deprecating style, but she became one of the seminary's leading board members.

Working with and knowing board members was one of the joys of my life. Every year I had a goal of personal contact with each board member, usually in their home or workplace. I spent considerable on-the-job time with executive-committee members and officers, and every week I met with the chair either face-to-face or by phone.

Many of the board members became lifelong friends. I performed the wedding for two of them and spoke at the funerals of several others. Shirley and I were touched by all of them, and our lives were enriched by their friendship in so many special ways.

An Expanded Lilly Grant

Following the success of the two earlier board development grants in the 1980s, I proposed to Lilly Endowment a multiyear grant through which Wesley would design and implement a trustee partner program involving the eight free-standing United Methodist Seminaries. The grant provided for an annual two-day gathering for the eight schools. Each school would bring its president, the chair of its board and two other board members. An atmosphere of openness, sharing, and learning from one another flowered among the schools. Board members from the various schools began to see each other as resources and would contact each other for information and advice between the annual meetings. The schools derived such benefit from the annual gathering that they continued them even after the grant period expired. That January conference still continues two decades later.

VIII. Fundraising-Institutional Advancement

One of the Wesley faculty members recently introduced me as the president who saved Wesley Seminary. As the story went, I did that by raising money. That is a myth based on truth, but it is not the whole truth. The community was trying to explain how the seminary suddenly experienced financial success rather than going broke. The myth had credibility because most people— inside and outside—assumed that the key to financial well-being of a school depends on how much money it could raise. Yes, we did raise more money than ever before. But no, you cannot save a school that way.

A fellow president used to tell me fairly often that if somebody would just donate $10 million to his seminary, it would be set for the future. That would have helped, of course, but would not entirely guarantee the future security of his school. Financial stability comes through a balance of multiple income sources. In spite of that reality, it is rare to find anyone within an institution who has any idea what percentage of its income is derived from fundraising and other sources.

The following chart correlates fundraising with Wesley's total income from fiscal 1981-82 through 1989-1990. Note the dramatic increase in the annual fund during the first two years, followed by modest growth afterwards with one slight decline.

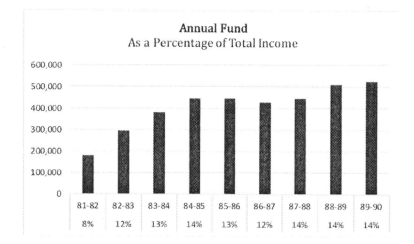

Another very telling number is the percentage of the seminary's total income that was produced by annual fundraising. Note that it grew from 8 percent in 1981-82 to 14 percent in 1988-89. The percentage contributed by the annual fund would increase but slowly during the 1990s. During that decade our gift income would increase primarily through foundation grants.

Fundraising is critical to the sustainability of most schools, but it has an impact that goes beyond just bringing in money. It has to do with building a constituency for the school—individuals and organizations such as churches, foundations, and denominations—who care about, advocate for, and invest in the school in a variety of ways. Fundraising in reality is "friend raising." I spent a significant amount of my time and energy making friends for the seminary. Friends are important, but those who are willing to invest themselves and their resources—money, contacts, influence, and advocacy—are vital.

The board of governors represented the key constituency of the seminary. The financial contributions of its members painted a critical picture of how well the seminary built and engaged its constituency. The following chart illustrates this dynamic.

Board Giving

	1981-82	1983-84	1988-89
To Annual Fund	$18,220	$93,557	$97,425
Members Giving	50%	90%	84%
Total Gifts by Board	$41,220	$104,107	$236,263
Members Giving	56%	90%	92%
Annual Fund by Board	10%	31%	19%

In 1981-82, only 50 percent of the board members made a gift to the annual fund and only 56 percent of them made a gift of any kind. They provided only 10 percent of the annual fund for that year.

1982-83, my first year at Wesley, showed a dramatic upswing. Board participation reached 90 percent and provided 31 percent of the annual fund. By 1988-89, 84 percent of the board members gave to the annual fund but that provided only 19 percent of the annual fund. Actually, that was a positive sign because we had begun to broaden our base and attract more donors.

I felt disappointed that 100 percent of the board members did not make a gift to the seminary. In the coming years we stressed 100 percent board-giving as a very important symbol of their investment in the seminary. As we approached an increasing number of foundations, many would ask what percentage of our board supported the seminary financially. We shared that story with the board, especially to newly-recruited members, as a critical responsibility. Within the next few years, the percentage of contributing members rose to 100 percent.

Slowdown in Annual Fund Growth

During the last half of the 1980s we continued to increase the annual fund each year, but not by much. Four factors were influential:

1. David McAllister-Wilson, who had taken over as director of development in 1987, reported a decline in leadership gifts—those above $5,000. Our major efforts in fundraising from 1982 forward focused on increasing Wesley Council gifts—$1,000 and above. The number increased every year and some moved into the leadership category. We were somewhat puzzled by the decline in leadership gifts. Council gifts continued to grow, but the leadership level fell off. The economy of the country was in decline during the

late 80s. We wondered how much it influenced the size of our gifts.

The major gift decline was a wakeup call. Significant growth in our annual fund would depend on increasing the number of leadership gifts. Consultant Tom Broce often reminded us that it takes as much time to identify and cultivate a $1,000 donor as a $5,000 donor, for only 20 percent of the return. We did recognize that Wesley's potential donor pool had more individuals who could and would make an entry gift of $1,000 than it had individuals willing and able to give $5,000. In the 1990s we would invest ever-increasing time and energy toward leadership givers.

2. In the late 1980s we were completing Wesley's first successful capital campaign. Most of our major donors to the campaign were also our most significant annual fund donors. Inevitably, some of their gifts to Wesley would migrate to the capital effort. We counted annual fund gifts as part of the capital campaign total, but we began to rethink our strategy for finding and sustaining larger annual gifts—otherwise we would level off in our overall fundraising efforts.

I remembered the remarkable success of my first years of fundraising. I wondered how to keep that dramatic increase going. I was seduced into thinking that fundraising was the key to solving an institution's financial ills, although in my more reflective moments, I knew that was not true. A decision about our student recruitment illustrated the point.

3. In the late 1980s we became increasingly aware of the importance of tuition income for growing and sustaining the seminary's income. Student recruitment took on ever-increasing importance. As a consequence, we decided to move the recruitment/admissions work into the institutional advancement office. That office already managed the public relations, communication, and alumni affairs, all of which enhanced recruiting efforts. The move had a downside, however—it shifted some of the staff's attention away from fundraising. The price we paid was raising less money in annual gifts.

4. Even after we renewed our fundraising efforts in the 1990s, competition for the time, energy and leadership of the director of institutional advancement persisted.

The focus of my efforts remained on fundraising and very little on recruitment. As I became increasingly aware of the need for larger annual gifts, I began to shift more of my attention toward those with leadership-giving potential. I did not, however, want to neglect our loyal and enthusiastic Wesley Council donors.

Obelia Scott Ross was the first African-American woman to graduate from Wesley. She loved the seminary and her connection to it. Obelia was in her 80s when I first met her and began to visit her modest home in Washington. We had intriguing conversations. She shared much about her experience at the seminary in the early 1970s. At my invitation she became a member of the Wesley Council, attended our banquets, and ultimately left her house to Wesley to invest in our urban ministry program.

Bishop Kulah, a Wesley graduate and current United Methodist bishop of Liberia, was visiting the seminary. I took him with me to call on Obelia. They were absolutely entranced with each other. I sat back and enjoyed their engaging conversation. The most difficult part was persuading them it was time for us to leave.

Obelia later wrote me a note: "I am ready for Heaven. Bishop Kulah has already given me a taste of it."

Capital Campaign

During my early years at Wesley a general awareness, particularly among board members, endured that the seminary had failed badly in its capital campaign during the 1970s. Considerable doubt existed regarding the seminary's capacity to raise significant capital gifts, even though our buildings were sorely in need of attention. Some of the new board members, taking note of our fundraising success, began to think we might be ready and able to launch a modest capital campaign.

Bill Klinedinst , a new board member, became co-chair of a campaign exploratory committee. He proposed that we launch a $4.7 million campaign to "fix" our facilities and generate scholarship money. He and Barbara Kettler, another new member, agreed to lead the campaign.

By the summer of 1988, the committee (a) announced we had reached our goal of $4.7 million and (b) immediately proposed we raise the goal to $5.2 million. By the spring of 1989, we had received $5.7 million in gifts. We had much to celebrate: the seminary's most successful campaign in its history, the completed building renovation project, and the funding of a new chair in evangelism. Morale was high.

Two significant gifts helped put us over the top. The Kresge Foundation made a grant of $450,000 toward the renovation of Kresge Academic Center and an unexpected bequest of $460,000 came in during the last year of the campaign.

IX. Financial Management

When I came to Wesley Seminary in 1982, I had some knowledge of financial conditions in America. Home mortgages had risen to 17 percent; inflation was up to 13 percent. Keeping pace with the cost of living grew more difficult by the year. What I did not realize was the impact these conditions were having on educational institutions. The seminary's budgets were dramatically out of balance. My first challenge was to stop the bleeding, fast—which we did.

But could we stay the course? That had more nuance than I first understood. "Balanced budget" referred to the operating budget. It was relatively easy to keep it in balance if you dip unaccountably into the endowment fund, but that was an act of self-deception. Wesley had practiced that deception to the point of draining the endowment tank almost dry. Once that happened, the seminary would be forced to borrow from outside and join some other schools on the slippery slope to extinction.

A President's Financial Knowledge

Capital projects, internal borrowing, endowment spending rates, operating reserves, investment management, the positive role of debt—all were new to me. Growing up on a farm I milked cows, sold milk, raised chickens, and sold eggs. Financing was simple— you needed to bring in more money than you spent. Financial management of an institution required more sophisticated knowledge. I had a lot to learn if the seminary was going to remain solvent.

A Gradual Change

Balancing the operating budget that first year was a major victory. It lifted our spirits and set us in a new direction. From that point forward, it was a matter of learning and putting the knowledge into practice. Our pace was slow, but it was steady. By the fall of 1984, we were able to stop internal borrowing to cover operational cash flow needs and start building reserves.

Capital projects that were not included in the operating budget proved more difficult to fund, but we managed. If we had a surplus in the operating budget, we used that. We also used undesignated bequests, but they were unpredictable. It took a few years before meeting our goal of including a line for capital costs in the operating budget.

In 1987, I reported to the board of governors these sources of our income for that year:

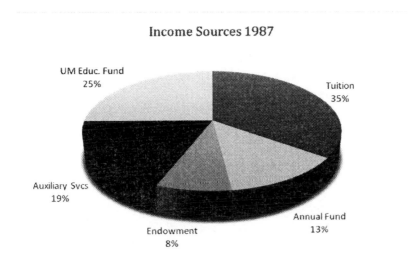

Income Sources 1987

UM Educ. Fund 25%

Tuition 35%

Auxiliary Svcs 19%

Endowment 8%

Annual Fund 13%

I also had to report that our financial future was uncertain. Enrollment was declining, thus reducing tuition income. The annual fund was increasing, but modestly. The United Methodist Church was about to change its distribution formula, and that would reduce our annual apportionment from the Ministerial Educational Fund (MEF)—the fund set up in the late 1960s to support the United Methodist theological schools.

Expense Budget

Salaries became a topic of considerable debate. Inflation had caused our faculty members to suffer during the dark days when the seminary had a shortage of funds. When the situation improved, we tried to atone for that by increasing their salaries 7 percent each year for a period of five years. In the late 1980s, however, with financial pressure on the income side and with a commitment to a balanced budget, a major discussion ensued. A study of other United Methodist seminaries showed that Wesley's salaries were lower among the senior ranks but higher for the junior ranks. (That was intentional, meant to help the younger members adjust to the real estate market in the Washington area.) After considerable discussion and debate, the board of governors and the administration decided that Wesley's 7 percent raises had to be brought into line with the other UM seminaries—down to the 4-5 percent range.

As for staff salaries, they had in general not kept up with faculty increases. I pushed for them to receive the same percentage increase as faculty. We instituted a staff salary pool, allocated on a percentage basis with the highest annual percentage raise going to those on the lowest pay scale.

All of us were disappointed, but no big resistance or protest arose. The Wesley community had long since learned to live with the seminary's financial struggles. They realized the seminary was on an upward track and that their compensation would benefit accordingly. Balancing the budget was still our top priority.

Thorny Issues

Two thorny issues appeared on the president's desk with regularity—food service and the bookstore. Early in my administration we had ceased running the food service with our own staff and contracted with a large company that specialized in serving educational institutions. Each change of manager by the company brought some improvement for a time, but then would come a decline. Complaints began to pile up, demanding the president's office take remedial action. The food service also lost money for lack of patrons. There was no profitable way to have a food service for our small community. We finally came to regard food service as a program cost that, like all our educational programs, required an ongoing subsidy. The main question became—how much subsidy was realistic?

The bookstore was another matter. Since moving to its Washington campus in 1958, Wesley had been operating its own bookstore. Traditionally run by a small staff, it did provide a special service to faculty and students. The faculty touted it as an educational arm with browsing opportunities for faculty and students alike. Eventually it became a social gathering place to discuss the latest seminary news—not always a positive contribution to the community.

The bookstore was also a management nightmare. The staff kept its own financial records, forcing the business office to maintain separate records suitable for integration into the seminary's budget. Balancing two sets of books became a source of endless confusion and conflict, often ending up on the president's desk in search of resolution.

Then came an unexpected gift. Cokesbury, the bookstore division of the United Methodist Publishing House, decided to take over all the United Methodist seminary campus bookstores. They paid a small rent for the space and footed the other bills. Not surprisingly, we heard murmurs about Wesley losing its own bookstore (they did not come from the president's office), but in due course the community grew to appreciate Cokesbury. It put its own person in charge, but retained the former manager in another position.

What none of us could know at that moment was that all Cokesbury stores were soon to be swept away by a technological tsunami. Wesley would end up with no bookstore at all—just personal computers with which to order from Amazon.

Investment Management

Before the 1980s, Wesley never had a large endowment—less than $2 million. Perhaps that is why it never developed a good investment strategy. In the 1970s and earlier, the endowment was managed by just one member of the board. When he retired, the funds were transferred to the trust department of a local bank. By 1986, we had repaid the funds borrowed from the endowment and built its assets up to $3.6 million. The bank's annual report to the seminary consisted of taking me out to lunch and recounting what a wonderful investment job they were doing.

A new chair of the board's investment committee suggested those funds would find a better home with an

142

investment management firm. The committee and I considered several firms and recommended E.F. Hutton.

For the next 10 years, E.F. Hutton moved us gradually away from our traditionally conservative strategy. They helped us transition to a total-return model and a withdrawal rate of 7 percent annually. (We had been thinking we could only spend the income from dividends and interest.) This new policy proved to be timely because the late 80s and the 90s turned into a raging bull market for equities.

The seminary's budgets were nonetheless tight during those years. Some of our projected budgets anticipated coming deficits, but we were always able to squeeze out a balanced operating budget by the end of the year. Counting the dollars up to the end of our fiscal year made June an annual stretch run for us.

That period of growth in finances, program, enrollment, and vision led us to pursue a larger endowment and to initiate a second capital campaign in the early 90s.

X. Care and Development of a President

I will forever be indebted to the Association of Theological Schools and the Association of United Methodist Theological Schools. They kept me abreast of developments in theological education and put me in touch with other seminary leaders who became supportive friends. They helped me become a better president in many ways.

Three years into my presidency at Wesley, I was invited to an ATS meeting. Leon Pacala, the executive director of the ATS, approached me during the meeting. "Well, Doug," he said, "I did not think you would make it at Wesley Seminary. In fact, I didn't think the seminary would survive. You have changed my mind. I think you and the seminary are going to do very well."

I was stunned. Before I could form a response, Leon asked how much time I was taking off each year. I fumbled a bit and said, "I don't know, exactly. Maybe a couple of weeks."

Leon proceeded to tell me that if I wanted to sustain my presidency for the long run, I should take a month's vacation every year and another month as study leave. I was stupefied. I had never taken off anywhere close to that much time, and there I was in the most important job of my life. I could not imagine being away that long. I did not say it, but I wondered how the school could manage without me. What would people think about such a long absence?

Leon was insistent. He asked permission to convey his suggestion to the chair of Wesley's board. I had no objection to that, but neither could I imagine being away for two months. I had long believed that serving as a seminary president was my primary calling in life. From my years on the farm, I grew up believing that success came from working as hard as you could for as long as you could. That surely included seminary presidents.

Wrong.

Leon had given me a wake-up slap in the face. From that "kairos" moment forward, I began to think about the kind of nourishment that it takes to keep one's body and spirit invigorated. I began to think more respectfully about expressions of sabbatical, renewal, retreat, and stewardship—all theological concepts concerning the rhythm and well-being of life. Maybe I should pay attention.

Not long after that Jim Waites, a good friend and dean of the Candler School of Theology, piqued my interest by sharing his positive experience of spending a summer in Cambridge, England. I discussed that with the chair of Wesley's board. He was most encouraging. (Maybe Leon's letter had made an impression on him.)

Jim helped Shirley and me track down an apartment at one of the colleges of Cambridge University. We spent two summer months there in 1987. I would start the day with a run, then read the International Herald Tribune. I concluded the morning reading philosophy and theology. In the afternoon I might read history or biography, maybe a novel in the evening. We strolled around the colleges and the gardens. We visited the libraries and the museums. We rode bikes around the town and saw plays. That summer began our love affair with Cambridge as our prime place of retreat.

Returning in the fall, I knew I was different than when I left. My mind was clearer. My body was rested. My imagination had expanded. My spirit felt deepened and enriched. What surprised me was how much reflection and mental work I did that summer about Wesley without even trying.

Leaving that first summer was very difficult for me. I felt guilty about such a long separation from the seminary. I wondered if the senior staff could manage without me. They fared quite well, thank you very much. I think they even enjoyed a sabbatical from me and my subtle pushing.

A side benefit that I had not anticipated was learning to trust my colleagues. They grew in their independence and competency. One summer I received a call from one

145

of the vice presidents announcing that they were redesigning my office, making it smaller, adding space for another office. Her final words were, "I hope you like it!" In fact, I did. It was a more appropriate use of space and my office actually functioned better.

 Other Opportunities

At the end of my second year at Wesley I attended the Theological Education Management, a three-week program developed by ATS and the Columbia University business school, funded by Lilly Endowment. The agenda covered all aspects of the administration of a theological school. My first exposure to a computer spreadsheet occurred there. I was blown away by it. Each of us designed a new management strategy for his or her school, put it into practice, then returned after six months to share the results with the whole group. That experience inspired me to take new directions as a seminary leader. Without a doubt, it was the best and most timely continuing education experience of my career. I developed many new colleagues and friends. Some, like Adolf Hansen, became career-long advisors and confidants.

The Association of United Methodist Theological Schools (AUMTS) provided opportunities to build close relationships with other United Methodist seminary leaders. Through support from the Division of Ordained Ministry of the United Methodist Church and its supportive director, Don Treese, AMUTS held an annual retreat which included spouses. Our quadrennial visit to theological schools around the world also included spouses. Don, with encouragement from Jim Waits and me, leased an apartment in Cambridge allowing each president to stay there for three months every four years. I learned from all of them and developed lasting friendships. I even met with one of the other presidents each year to share notes about our budgets and financial-planning strategies.

Other Boards

During my tenure, I served on a number of not-for-profit boards. I usually chose small, progressive organizations whose missions I believed in, and from whom I could learn and provide benefit to Wesley. In each of them I ended up serving as chair of the board.

Plowshares Institute enabled Wesley to become a part of its innovative globalization program.

The Appalachia Ministry Educational Resource Center (AMERC), in cooperation with seminaries, provided educational immersions in Appalachia for seminary students. It also developed and led an Appalachian immersion for the Wesley faculty and board members.

A Christian Ministry in the National Parks (ACMNP) provided summer ministry opportunities for students in the national parks.

In Trust worked with seminaries on governance and board development and published a widely-read magazine for seminary board members and administrators. In 1992 Wesley Seminary was featured on the cover of the magazine, the first time the cover had been printed in color.

By a fluke, I was elected to the Advisory Neighborhood Council (ANC), a unique political structure that dealt with neighborhood issues and gave advice to the Washington City Council. That, along with being selected to participate in Leadership Washington, exposed me to insights about the District of Columbia. My political career was short-lived, however; an AU student defeated me in the next election.

In many respects a president's life is spent on the road—serving on boards, speaking, raising money, attending meetings, and such. Those activities had many direct and indirect benefits that accrued to Wesley, but scheduling them around office business, campus events, committee work, and chapel became a high-wire balancing act. I never left without a twinge of guilt wondering if that trip was really necessary. The staff had fun teasing me about leaving just when things were getting hot on the home front. However, the board of governors always supported my outside involvements, as did my colleagues.

Presidential Time and Focus

I struggled with the issues of focus and use of my time. Another seminary president friend of mine, Robert Cooley, turned on a light for me one day. "Doug," he said, "the central focus of a seminary president's job is institutional advancement. Everything you do should be guided by advancing the seminary toward fulfilling its mission and providing the resources necessary to sustain that mission into the future." Bob's words stayed with me. Every morning I asked myself what are the most important things I need to do today—on campus or off—to advance the mission of Wesley Seminary. I also admit those words occasionally made me feel as though a slave-driving tyrant was controlling all that I did.

Balancing between a full-time focus on "institutional advancement" and maintaining personal health, vitality, and well-being makes the high-wire act even more challenging. The position of president easily leads one to assume he/she must know it all and do it all. Presidents need help. The board and candid, supportive colleagues are keys. A board that hires and can fire a president needs to develop a process to support a president and pay attention to his/her well-being.

Considering Other Positions

The Wesley board always supported me. I never felt skittish about approaching them with ideas, suggestions, or personal requests. But near the end of the 1980s, I struggled with a serious personal issue.

In a period of just two years, I was presented with four job possibilities—two seminary presidencies, a university presidency, and CEO of a theological agency. Each one held some attraction for me, but I felt pangs of guilt for considering them. They all offered a higher salary—two of them considerably higher—but money was not the real issue. I was never the highest-paid president among the United Methodist seminaries— usually somewhere in the middle. In fact, I suggested the board not give me a large raise; I wanted my income to be commensurate with others at Wesley.

Helen Smith had become chair of the Wesley board. She mobilized the executive committee to let me know in no uncertain terms they wanted me to stay. They recognized my concerns about not building housing equity and having a good retirement program. Under her leadership, the committee set up a deferred income plan, augmented by the seminary, to enhance my retirement program. I could also make personal contributions to it. They were even willing to consider our purchase of a home.

Those new opportunities were enticing, and I wrestled with each one. Shirley and I had many conversations about them. To go or not to go? She and she alone knew that it wasn't really about the money or the house or the retirement plan. It was about challenge. I feasted on challenge, new opportunities, and the next big idea. With a dose of homespun Tennessee philosophy, she settled the issue when she said to me: "Get your head out of the clouds and keep your feet on the ground. Isn't it better to dig in and make a long-term contribution?"

Revelation comes in many forms and words!

Leadership and Change: A President's Story

Phase III

A New Decade

1990-1995

A Feeling Turn

During my graduate studies, Shirley and I had a life-changing opportunity to spend a year in Germany at the University of Hamburg. Driving a Volkswagen bug with travel book in hand *(Europe on Five Dollars a Day)*, we tried to visit as many countries as our free time and budget permitted. One trip took us to Nice via Switzerland and across the French Alps. It was a roller-coaster ride that left us wondering if the mountains would go on forever. We would wind our way down one mountain into a valley with the inevitable village, ascend the next mountain, and hope to see water. Nope. So down we would go to the next village-in-the-valley, up the next mountain, and look again. Nope. Another mountain would stretch before us. So down we'd go and up we'd go, again and again. Finally, when it was nearly sunset of the second day, we topped the last mountain and beheld the beautiful Mediterranean Sea and the lights of Nice twinkling in the twilight.

Our Wesley Seminary journey across the 1980s felt somewhat like that trip across the Alps. Up we'd go and down we'd go. Each little village of success had its own special charm, but there was always another mountain to climb. Perhaps most of us fantasize about reaching some Utopian pinnacle where we can relax, let off pressure, and take the time to enjoy success. The Wesley community had climbed many mountains and reached heights never before achieved. While we did not expect Utopia, we could be forgiven for hoping that as we reached the end of the decade, maybe the 1990s would be easier. Nope. We saw the same thing—more valleys, more mountains to climb. I did not feel tired or discouraged, but I did take a deep breath and wonder just how far that range of challenges really did stretch.

I. Assessing the 1980s

We scheduled several different planning sessions. The board's Executive Committee had a full day's meeting with the administration to examine the seminary's finances for the future. The board and faculty had a one-day retreat to review the self-study and the feedback from the accrediting agencies. We met with the bishops and their staffs of three annual conferences to explore how we could work together toward better preparing our students for ministerial leadership. As president, I used my reports to the board to summarize our accomplishments, identify the issues facing us, and suggest strategies for going forward.

We had followed the long-range plan we developed in the early 1980s, and it had served us well, as shown by these achievements.

- We stabilized the seminary financially and balanced the budget each year
- The endowment grew from less than $1 million to more than $4 million
- The annual fund increased steadily each year
- Wesley's first successful capital campaign came in well above its $5.1 million goal
- The Kresge Academic Center and the library underwent major renovations
- Enrollment remained steady
- The seminary's diversity—students, faculty, staff, and board—increased
- A major self-study was completed, and Wesley received reaccreditation
- A major revision of the curriculum focused on serving the church through preparing its ministerial leadership
- Our global immersion program had significant impact on the faculty, board, and students

- Fourteen new faculty members were hired, changing 50 percent of the core faculty, with a net increase of 2 ½ positions
- Wesley's sabbatical policy was upgraded to provide more time off as well as providing junior faculty earlier leave than before
- Four new programs were added: student pastor track, urban ministry, deaf ministries, and global immersions
- A unique Center for Religion and the Arts was set into motion
- Student aid was increased from 17 percent to 30 percent of tuition
- Half of the board of governors were new

Many Mountains

Money had not been the only issue facing Wesley in 1982, but it had been at the core. Eight years later, that was still the case. In some ways, the financial mountain actually seemed higher in 1990. Success had led us to expect more of ourselves; we set ever-higher goals. That $10 million fantasy gift, meanwhile, had not shown up.

At the beginning of the new decade I reported to the board:

- The enrollment headcount was almost 400, but the number of tuition hours was static at about 6500
- Tuition income continued to grow as a percentage of the budget, while other income areas slipped
- MEF was declining as a percentage of the income budget
- Annual fund was increasing, albeit slowly
- We had no regular annual income to cover facilities or capital costs
- The seminary was under-capitalized with only a $4 million endowment

154

- Over the previous four years, income to annual budget had increased 7 percent annually, but expenses had increased 8.7 percent. To cover that shortfall, we would need to increase our income by $65-100,000 dollars annually
- Budget projections for the next five years showed annual deficits rising above $500,000 by 1995
- It was unclear how the seminary should relate to the church with regard to enrollment and appropriate education for ministerial preparation
- We had to replace three of the four senior administrators—academic dean, dean of students, and business manager
- Additional staffing was needed in development and admissions

Proposed Strategies

The most obvious solutions to our needs seemed to be (a) an increase in enrollment, (b) an increase in tuition rate, and (c) an annual increase in funds raised for the endowment. However, each of those ideas had a downside. Recruiting more students would necessitate new and extended staff efforts, plus closer partnering with the church. Increasing tuition would put greater financial pressure on students, forcing them to borrow more. There was also a limit to the number of newly-minted pastors our constituent churches could absorb. We began promoting fresh educational programs with the potential to attract other students—an MTS degree for laity and a DMin for active pastors.

The administration, board, and faculty—together and separately—grappled with these issues for two years. We had become accustomed to balanced budgets, higher investments in our programs, increased compensation and benefits for faculty and staff, and updates to our facilities. No one wanted to retrench. Although 1990-91 felt like a turning point in the wrong direction, four strategies eventually began to emerge. Each would require some change and some new initiatives.

A. Ministry 2000

During a board meeting in the late 80s, lay member Clare Stanford interrupted the proceedings. He blurted out: "Mr. Chairman and Mr. President! I have a growing concern about Wesley Seminary. Do we really care about our involvement and service to the United Methodist Church, or are we just working on our own agenda, hoping they will support us?" There was silence in the room. Clare went on: "I think we should invite the bishops from our key conferences to come to Wesley for a serious discussion about how we can work together more effectively."

I wondered if Clare did not understand the workload of a bishop. It would be hard enough for any of them to find time to spare for such discussions. Certainly we couldn't expect all four of them to come to the campus for a joint meeting. But as I scanned the room, I noticed many lay members nodding their heads in agreement. A few of them even said, "Yes!" out loud.

Clare moved that the president, acting for the seminary, should invite the bishops to Wesley in the spring. The motion carried unanimously. I had no choice.

Honestly, to my surprise, all four bishops from our key conferences accepted—Baltimore, Central Pennsylvania, Peninsula, and Virginia. They met with us that spring, and we developed a cooperative project called Ministry 2000. They all agreed to support the project in their conferences and to return for an annual meeting each

156

spring for the next three years to assess progress and review action plans. (So much for my private doubts.)

Here are the goals set for the project:
1. Focus the church and seminary on ministerial leadership for the 21st century
2. Stress the role of the local church in enlisting candidates for ministry, and provide resources to assist them in this task
3. Develop financial support for theological education at Wesley Seminary

The group agreed on these cooperative activities:
- Bishops would serve on the steering committee
- Seminary representatives would have regular meetings with conference cabinets and Boards of Ordained Ministry
- Each annual conference would establish a liaison committee, and lay advisory and clergy advisory committees
- Congregations throughout the conferences would devote a Ministry Sunday to emphasize the call to ministry
- Each annual conference would hold "call-to-ministry" events.

This vision was lofty and idealistic. For those plans to reach fruition would require deep commitment on the part of many people in the churches and the seminary. The major effort of organizing all the activities fell to the Wesley staff. Because we had not been geared up to handle that additional workload, not all the actions were activated nor were all the goals achieved. The huge effort, however, did raise the consciousness of both church and seminary with regard to their mutual responsibilities toward those who were called into ministry. Identifying and supporting those who sought to answer the call was a duty to be shared.

The project's goal—to build a stronger relationship between the seminary and four annual conferences—did not fit easily into the traditional activities of the seminary's development and admissions offices. That effort would move us into uncharted territory.

Clare was right, and he pushed the right buttons.

Despite what we proclaimed publicly, the seminary could easily have gone its own way, expecting support from the church while investing only the semblance of cooperative effort. The churches could have taken a similar position, strictly minding their own affairs and expecting the seminary to produce ready-made pastors who could hit the ground running. Ministry 2000 compelled church and seminary to buck tradition and explore ways to work together.

The seminary invested heavily in developing materials, arranging meetings, and building relationships. Although payoff was not immediately obvious, the effort had a long-term impact on the seminary and the conferences. It forced the seminary to think about its relationship with its constituent churches and how best to serve them. It heightened visibility of the seminary within the conferences and congregations.

<u>Early Results</u>

At the December, 1991, executive committee meeting, David McAllister-Wilson reported that more than 350 churches had requested Ministry 2000 materials. He estimated that at least one-third of the churches in the four annual conferences had held Ministry Sundays. As a result of that and 50,000 brochures that were sent out, some 160 prospects returned cards expressing their interest in becoming United Methodist seminary students. Some prospective donors even emerged from the congregations.

Ministry 2000 served as a model for the other United Methodist theological schools. In the spring of 1993, the Association of United Methodist Theological Schools (AUMTS) launched Agenda 21, a three-year project in which each of its 13 schools would work with four annual conferences in its region. Each school would develop its own working relationship with these conferences, but the basic approach would follow the model Wesley had created.

B. Expanding Staff in Development and Admissions

Pressure had been growing in development and admissions. Two years earlier, we had combined the two offices under Vice President David McAllister-Wilson. In addition to traditional student recruitment and admissions work, his staff took on public relations and communications, plus fundraising. Student recruitment tended to win the race for their time and attention. It was daily duty, working directly with interested students while under pressure to meet enrollment goals.

David did a great job of organizing and energizing the two offices, but he also admitted that development suffered most for lack of concentrated time and energy. Fundraising requires locating prospects, cultivating them, and then finally asking them for a gift. That calls for strong personal initiative to get off campus and make contacts. Feeling comfortable asking people for money is not everyone's cup of tea. It requires a certain confidence level about oneself along with an affinity for those who may become donors. Many development officers feel more comfortable working from a distance (events, sending materials) than face-to-face.

Acutely aware of our financial situation, I worried that we were slipping in the fundraising department. Justification of my fears showed in the too-modest growth of the annual fund, coupled with a noticeable decline in leadership gifts. I still assumed that fundraising was the key to Wesley's long-term financial health. Consequently, I stayed on the road a considerable amount of the time contacting, cultivating, and soliciting individual donors as well as a growing number of foundations.

Suddenly the new demands of Ministry 2000 fell onto the shoulders of a staff already worn thin. David pulled no punches in telling the board what his two offices could and could not do. In a nutshell, he said they could maintain the status quo—period. They could not expand their services as they felt pushed to do.

He got the message across. Even with a budget so tight that it pinched, the board authorized one additional staff member in each of the two departments.

C. Restrain Expense Growth

Cutting expenses or curbing their growth is difficult. It felt impossible to do either one while proposing to launch a project the size of Ministry 2000 and a capital campaign that required an outside consulting firm plus adding a part-time staff person in planned giving. Now we were about to add two new staff for development and admissions.

Our budget projections for the next five years already predicted growing deficits. I felt compelled to take a hard look at every expense area and determine where we could make cuts and reinvest the savings into the needed growth areas. It became a serious challenge to keep morale stable while asking for sacrifices.

In January of 1991 I met with the faculty for our annual budget session. We began with a projected $254,000 deficit for the coming year. We looked at various options for dealing with the problem. On April 30, in a memorandum to the faculty, I summarized the work we had done and the 1991-92 budget proposal I was taking to the board.

To the Faculty:

Since January we have analyzed and struggled with next year's budget and the tightness of our financial situation. We are particularly concerned about the trends which are pushing us toward a structural deficit and forcing us into decisions that spend part of our future resources and neglect some areas such as capital repairs on our physical plant. Program and department managers have trimmed their budgets. The administrative council has explored various alternative scenarios. The board finance committee made its recommendations. Finally, the vice president for finance and I worked on the remaining tough decisions—there were some painful choices. I thought you would be interested in where we propose to increase income and cut expenses to erase the $254,000. [I specified dollar amounts in the proposed line items increasing income and cutting expenses.] I am also including some additional background financial information.

The board will receive this proposal to assist them in determining the final budget.

Some Factors Built into the Budget

- 5% across the board increase in faculty salaries. However, the line item for faculty salaries increased by 8.4% because of increased rank for two faculty

- 9% increase in adjunct faculty budget
- 5% general increase for staff, although total staff cost went up 5.8%
- 5% increase for administrators

Some Basic Concerns

- Again we balanced our budget by increasing our income projections more than was prudent
- We are budgeting for 6900 tuition hours, but have not achieved that level since 1984-85
- We are dangerously high in foundation grants projections and spending current ones too rapidly
- Our annual fund projections are creeping up while we plan to undertake a major capital campaign effort
- We are staffing for greater efforts in enlistment and fundraising, but there is a cost/benefit risk. Will the investment in new staff produce that much more income?
- We are investing in creative new programs and adding quality, but our costs are rising faster than our income.

Other Data

The following are some data from other comparable ATS seminaries. One quickly recognizes that Wesley is more tuition-dependent and endowment-poor.

Income Sources	Wesley	Other ATS Schools
Tuition and Fees	40.0%	24.6%
Endowment	7.7%	22.5%
MEF (Church)	18.7%	16.5%
Gifts/Grants	17.5%	17.5%
Other Income	1.0%	6.4%
Auxiliary	15.0%	12.3%

Expenditures	Wesley	Other ATS Schools
Admin/General	25.3%	25.8%
Instruction	37.2%	35.8%
Library	5.8%	6.2%
Facilities	7.3%	8.6%
Student Aid	10.7%	11.1%
Transfers	2.5%	1.3%
Auxiliary	10.8%	10.9%

I am very open to discussing all of this information in greater detail.

Douglass Lewis
President

Faculty Response

The entire faculty expressed understanding of the seminary's financial distress and were willing to make sacrifices. There was, however, a marked lack of enthusiasm about one particular item. Budget discussions had included the possibility of adding a fifth course to each faculty member's teaching load. For those who were already receiving extra compensation for teaching a fifth course, that would equate to a salary cut. We scrapped that idea.

The faculty was also aware of the proposed percent reduction in faculty raises (from 6 percent to 5 percent). There was understanding and acceptance, but they wanted the reductions to be fair and include staff and administration. We made it so.

A primary concern of the faculty was to continue to be kept aware of budget plans and have a voice in future planning and decisions. They suggested a reinstitution of the strategic planning committee and perhaps a faculty representative to the administrative council.

At the time we did not refer to this discussion and decision-making process as "shared governance." In fact, it was just that. My primary job was governance—developing and facilitating planning and decision-making processes that enabled the seminary to fulfill its mission and maintain its financial sustainability. To be "shared governance," key parts of the community—staff, faculty, administration, and board—would need to feel included, knowledgeable, and influential. This delicate dance was never perfectly achieved, but we came close enough to maintain good morale. Faculty and staff remained committed to giving their very best to Wesley Seminary. I was grateful to every one of them.

D. Capital Campaign

Wesley was under-capitalized. Everyone knew it. The endowment was small and it produced less than 8 percent of the annual operational income. We had stabilized the shaky financial condition of 1982 with less than $1 million in endowment. For the remainder of the decade, we produced a balanced budget annually and achieved modest growth in the endowment to bring it above $4 million by 1990. But to achieve the status, influence, and the quality we wanted, the seminary needed a more secure financial base.

Endowments usually grow slowly through investments, bequests, and some designated gifts from individuals. We wanted to jump-start the process through a capital campaign for endowment. The time seemed right to launch a serious effort to do that.

Wesley had no history of receiving a number of large financial gifts, either in the annual fund or in capital efforts. A consultant we hired insisted that Wesley could raise $10 million over a two-year period. That sounded fantastic, but I wondered if we could climb such a mountain. I will share more of the details of the campaign in a later section.

Someone asked me once: "As a seminary president, how often do you think about and work on fundraising?" My answer was always, "Every day!" Now I found myself thinking, "Every night" as well.

II. Enrollment—a Huge Surprise

Financially speaking, 1991-92 looked like another steep mountain to climb. It was too early to see if our new strategies would take us over the top yet again, so about all we could do was keep our heads down and push forward. Then, to our complete surprise, enrollment took a 26 percent leap in the fall of 1991. Wesley Seminary received, in effect, a $250,000 bonus—or was it a permanent raise?

We had no way to predict that enrollment would reach the 600-student level within five years. Curiously, the number of tuition hours would lag behind the enrollment surge, which could be seen as an anomaly. Actually, it was a signal that a new era had begun. The makeup of our student body was changing so dramatically that we would soon be compelled to make adjustments. The students would be considerably older than before. They would have family responsibilities and jobs that put limits on the amount of time they had for classroom work and study. They would be more inclined to commute to the campus than live in a dormitory. They would need to borrow more for their education than their predecessors.

The following statistics reveal these trends:

Year	MDiv	MRE/MA	MTS	DMin	Others	Total	Tuit. Hrs
90-91	237	17	44	68	41	407	6740
91-92	293	19	63	73	64	512	7800
92-93	314	27	58	96	76	571	7909
93-94	330	31	55	110	78	604	7780
94-95	316	31	52	112	90	601	7785

These increases affected all of us in all departments. It created excitement, affirmed our intense enlistment efforts, relieved a budget stress for the year, and solidified our continuing work with the annual conferences through the Ministry 2000 project.

It also created some challenges. Required courses were overflowing. Faculty members had more advisees than they could handle. Pressure for more financial aid increased. We were scratching our heads wondering if the changes would be long-lasting. Should we adjust our plans for the future? The board of governors called for an in-depth look into these issues and what actions might be required. Subsequent discussions among board members, faculty, and staff proved to be quite revealing and helped us adapt to the changing times. The following are some of the discussion points and ideas about key issues that we considered:

The Potential Pool of Students

The number of United Methodist MDiv students appeared to be falling in direct proportion to the decline in the number of UM churches. Wesley was perceived as an open, diverse, and attractive seminary for students from other denominations. Almost 40 percent of the student body were non-UM. Enrollment in the MDiv degree, which had long been the core of Wesley's program, was flat or declining all across ATS schools. Many of them were turning to other degree programs in order to shore up their enrollments. Wesley joined the trend with increased emphasis on its DMin and Masters programs.

Competition

Wesley's reputation and visibility had increased throughout the 1980s. Ministry 2000 created a new connection to our close-in annual conferences. Ministry Sundays in local churches raised a call to ministry at the grassroots level. Our investment in marketing, recruitment and admissions was bearing fruit. Even the amount of financial aid available, though still less than we needed, had increased significantly.

Educational Capacity

How flexible could the educational program become? Would we offer multiple options—evening and week-end courses, week intensives, off-site courses and programs? How many students and programs could we handle with our current faculty? Were our educational and campus facilities adequate and attractive?

Quality and Program Focus

There had been a strong push on the recruitment and budgetary side to bring in as many students as possible without loss of quality. We all owned the mission of preparing the next generation of the church's leaders. Our relationship with churches through Ministry 2000 and the design of our curriculum each reflected our commitment to turning out effective pastoral leaders.

Uncertainty

All those present for the discussions recognized that we could not be certain about future enrollment. We did recognize that Wesley was a tuition-dependent school—about 40-45 percent of our income would continue to come from tuition and fees. Without a steady enrollment and a significant number of tuition hours, the seminary would face serious financial problems.

International Students

When I arrived on the Wesley campus in 1982, we had a cadre of international students, mainly from West African countries. Their financial situations were similar in that each of them had some assistance from their home churches. Wesley helped too, but only during their first year. After that, most of them were forced into generating support from local sources because immigration regulations did not allow them to work without a permit, which was very difficult to obtain.

Many of them turned immediately to the new president. Given my interest and commitment to the globalization of theological education, I tried to help. Those efforts backfired. Unless I could help all of them, the ones left out would feel unfairly treated—and rightfully so. By the same token, our globalization efforts also made things worse without solving anything. Whenever I traveled to other countries to teach, speak, or lead an immersion group, I would inevitably meet individuals with great potential for leadership in their home country and church. Having an educational opportunity in the United States, particularly at Wesley, could significantly enhance their capacities. When I returned to campus, the staff would tentatively ask, "How many new international students did you recruit on this trip?"

I was not the only culprit. One of our board members donated $30,000 to set up a special program for international students. Under that plan, a congregation would take a student into its fold, providing necessary support. It was a noble idea, but it generated an unsustainable workload for the seminary staff. They had to recruit sponsoring congregations, match them with students, and deal with whatever issues might arise between the two parties. Some pairings worked well, while others were disappointing.

Much later we did experience one notable success when a Wesley supporter, out of the blue, gave us $400,000 to support African students and programs. His generosity led to the establishment of a special DMin program for faculty members from African seminaries to focus on teaching skills and advanced scholarship in their fields.

My biggest frustration with our international students was that most of them wanted to stay in America. I understood their motivation, but it went counter to our goal of preparing them for leadership roles in their home churches.

Korean Initiative

Our most successful program for international students came out of our Korean initiative, thanks to the remarkable Kyunglim Shin Lee. I first hired her as dean of community life. She developed into a recruiter and fund-raiser extraordinaire and went on to create a successful scholarship program for Koreans. She influenced many of them to attend Wesley, including some who were already living in the United States. She helped them find positions in Korean parishes not only in the Washington area but all around the country. Later, she initiated specially-designed international DMin programs and managed dozens of Korean pastors who enrolled in them.

In the early stages of Kyunglim's work to enlist Korean students, she and I met with Dae Hee Park, the first Korean graduate from Wesley back in the 1970s. He suggested and then worked with us to establish an endowed scholarship program for Korean students at Wesley. Kyunglim subsequently played the lead role in raising almost $3 million for that program.

III. Planning and Management

Serving as president of Wesley Seminary was challenging, but it was fun. To switch from the mountain-climbing metaphor, it was akin to negotiating a swift river in a canoe. There were times when the river ran straight and there was little to do but paddle. Then would come a sudden turn into furious white water. Survival became a matter of planning the safest route and somehow holding to the long-range course without smashing into boulders all around us.

It was a tricky river all the way. Each of the three primary planning groups—the board, the administrative council, and the faculty—had its own processes. My job was to keep them synchronized and moving in the same direction.

For several months, the administrative council and the joint faculty-administrative committee had been working on the draft of a summary planning document. In February of 1992 the board, the faculty, and the administration came together for a Friday-Saturday retreat at Ocean City, Maryland. That was a first for us. The retreat focused on this planning document:

Mission Statement

"Wesley Seminary is a graduate theological school of the United Methodist Church. It serves the mission of the church by educating people for leadership in various forms of ministry. It is the church's community of learning, which provides theological leadership on issues facing the church and the world."

Strategic Vision

"To accomplish its mission, Wesley will focus on the following primary goals:

- Develop new educational programs and paradigms on congregational life and pastoral leadership
- Build a community of learning and formation for ministry in the midst of growing diversity
- Build an effective team for the overall management of the seminary and its programs
- Build a long term development program
- Increase the quality and effectiveness of the board of governors and other advisory groups
- Increase the quality of the student body through selection from a larger and more qualified pool and better retention"

Barbara Taylor from the staff of the Association of Governing Boards served as our facilitator. She divided us into small, mixed groups. Each one had the assignment to address two priority goals, specify activities that could help realize them, and steps the board could take to help. We then considered what the board would need in the way of tools—e.g., information, skills, and processes.

For each of us—board, faculty, and administration—that retreat provided a better understanding of a common vision for the seminary and what we needed to do toward fulfilling it.

Operational Plan

The mission, vision, and strategic goal document that came out of that retreat guided our efforts for the next few years. As an implementing strategy, each administrative council members wrote an annual operational plan listing objectives that would enable the seminary to fulfill the strategic goals in each of their areas. Each of us wrote an executive summary of our previous year's operational work. That, along with the coming year's operational plan, was sent to the board of governors and discussed with them during the fall meeting.

Steering the seminary boat did not always go smoothly. In spite of my struggle to put together the right administrative leadership team, some pieces were occasionally missing, misplaced, or malfunctioning. Overall, though, I felt we were navigating the river quite well. We had a clear understanding of where we wanted to go. We had an ongoing planning process to guide our work. We were achieving many of our goals and showed tangible results in enrollment, creative educational programs, a growing diverse community, successful fundraising, and a growing recognition of Wesley as an innovative, successful theological school.

IV. Senior Administrators

Presidents make decisions—lots of them. It comes with the territory. Every workday seems to bring with it the need for something to be resolved. Mostly, the issues are small and easy to handle. Others might require staff meetings to sort them out, and some might even have ramifications of interest to the community at large. The hardest ones—head and shoulders above all others—are personnel decisions.

Personnel decisions are more complicated. They carry more risk, and their consequences, for better or worse, are likely to extend well into the future. When key people are involved, the level of difficulty shoots up dramatically, along with the level of importance. Even further, most individuals have a coterie of supporters, which gives personnel decisions a built-in capacity to spread outward very quickly. I usually found myself in the middle trying to balance differences, encourage openness, seek common ground, and sometimes protect those who could be hurt.

My closest colleagues—my working partners—were the senior administrators with whom I shared the responsibility of leading and managing the seminary. Building that team required careful choices—finding, hiring, supervising, and sometimes changing members of the team. Many turned out to be extraordinary individuals whose talents and dedication helped transform the seminary.

My most difficult decisions came when I decided to make a change in someone's responsibilities or continuance in the position. When Douglas Cooney, our business manager, retired in 1990, we went through a two-year period finding a replacement who had strong financial capabilities, finally landing Judy Stanfield. Traditionally the business manager had also supervised other administrative offices. Covering that responsibility and managing the finances was a stretch. We really needed two people—one in finance and one in administrative supervision.

Risky Decision

I developed a somewhat surprising but risky solution that involved David McAllister-Wilson. David had been an important player in the administrative team at Wesley since his first year as a student, which happened to be my first year as president. He had served effectively as a development assistant, director of development, and vice president for institutional advancement. During his five years as vice president he reorganized and transformed our admission/recruitment and development offices. He was insightful about the issues facing the seminary in these areas, and he continually posed new possibilities to advance the seminary.

I was aware that David had a growing concern about his future and a desire for more responsibility and leadership opportunities. I decided to name him executive vice president and expand his responsibilities to cover those internal administrative areas while retaining oversight for development and admission/recruitment.

I was not entirely happy with my decision, however. Our fundraising was still underperforming, even though we were expanding our staff and opening a new area in planned giving and capital development. David had a gift for relationship building and cultivation of donors. Giving him more internal administrative responsibility would

174

only reduce his time and energy he could put into external relations. I was also not sure that day-to-day supervision of in-house services was the best use of his talents. To assuage my anxiety, I determined to spend more of my own time on external development work.

Painful Decision

My most difficult personnel decision came later. Our academic dean's five-year contract was coming up for renewal. His scholarship was highly respected, and he pushed hard to strengthen our curriculum by adding new elements to the core program. He and I shared a commitment to the seminary as the primary educational arena for preparing strong leadership for the church.

I had a deep respect for him as a churchman, theologian, faculty member, and friend. However, he and I had significantly different administrative styles. After a long struggle personally, I became convinced that his major gifts were as a theologian and teacher, not as an administrator. I felt his best contribution to Wesley would be as a tenured member of the faculty, not as an academic administrator. I knew that my decision about the matter would have significant impact on the seminary and on him personally.

In May of that year, my mother died rather suddenly, just two weeks after her 90th birthday. I flew to Tennessee and reached her hospital bedside the very hour she breathed her last. During the following days, even in the midst of arranging the funeral and mingling with hometown folks, my thoughts continually returned to the issue of the dean. I remembered that my mother, reflecting on her years as a dietician in a state mental hospital and a home economics teacher, had always said that you cannot avoid hard problems. Facing them is difficult but the wiser course of action for the long term.

After my return to Wesley, I continued to deliberate in private. Normally, I consulted with members of the faculty and the board in the case of high-level appointments, though official policy did not require that I do so. In this case I did not. After a few days, I went to the dean's office and told him I had decided not to extend his appointment as dean beyond the coming year. He was visibly shocked and immediately volunteered to resign as dean.

A president must take responsibility for deciding what is right and necessary for the community, and for taking the necessary action to bring about the needed results. Failure to do so can be to the detriment of the institution.

The opportunity for members of the community to have appropriate input in matters vital to the institution has a strong effect on morale and commitment of community members. Although we tried to practice shared governance at Wesley, there was always some ambiguity concerning who had authority to make what decisions. I have long wondered if my decision bypassed an opportunity to strengthen shared governance.

I don't doubt, however, that I directly addressed a critical issue that no one had quite known how to handle except to talk about it around the edges. I did solve the problem, but my presidency took a hit.

Fallout

The news spread like a wildfire among the faculty. When I also suggested that I would appoint a faculty member as acting dean, many of the faculty members considered my intent was to make that appointment permanent. They saw that as yet another unilateral decision. That brought the number of rifts I had to contend with up to two.

Anger and widespread consternation ensued. No one seemed happy with my actions. I received a letter of sharp criticism from Bruce Birch, one of the most insightful and thoughtful members of the faculty, a man who had always supported me. He informed me that I had violated Wesley's traditional procedures for handling matters involving personnel.

I took a deep breath, reflected on my action, and acknowledged that I had made an egregious error. I then visited another influential faculty member—this one a strong supporter of the dean. I listened carefully to his outrage and condemnation of me. I confessed that I had made a serious mistake and apologized. Eventually, he and I were able to discuss what should be done next.

I then called a meeting of the entire faculty and apologized for the process mistake I had made. I also had a number of conversations with the dean himself. We made an effort to calm the waters and find a solution that would honor his work as dean while still affirming the need for change.

The final decision was to extend his deanship by two years and give him a one-semester sabbatical. Before the expiration of that extension, however, he accepted a very good offer to serve on the faculty of a university divinity school.

I survived the crisis and subsequently regained my leadership footing with the board, the faculty, and the community. The respect and support I had built over a decade of service at the seminary proved to be a reservoir of trust and confidence in my leadership that helped us through that difficult period.

I was later asked if I worried about making a wrong decision. The answer is no. Decisions have to be made, and they cannot all be right. The best anyone can do is try to make good decisions, then work hard to make them right.

V. Board Development

I believed from the beginning of my tenure that a strong and effective board of governors would be essential to making Wesley a leading seminary. I therefore invested significant time and energy in its development. By 1990, the board had changed dramatically in its makeup and its governing capacity. Several factors were vital in that transformation.

Makeup

An early change in the bylaws allowed us to recruit a more diverse membership. During the 1980s, the 50-50 composition of laity-clergy became two-thirds laity. Several members brought financial management and investment expertise to the board. All of them were committed to sound governance and to more effective planning. In addition, our capital campaigns and the annual fund were the beneficiaries of increased contributions from many of the new members.

Education of the Board

A new board did not spring forth quickly. The quality and commitment of its members were the bedrock, but they had to invest time and resources to gain a better understanding of seminary education and management. Grants from Lilly Endowment kick-started that process and provided long-term board education for the Wesley board.

Retreats with the Faculty

In 1990 we began a series of annual retreats for the board and faculty, as well as administration. These events allowed us to meet in a relaxed environment to exchange ideas face-to-face. We worked together identifying the critical issues facing the seminary and setting strategic goals for dealing with these issues. Out of these sessions came a common vision for the future.

In February of 1992 we had one of our most significant retreats. Its focus on important issues led to the adoption of a strategic planning document for the seminary which included (a) Mission Statement, (b) Strategic Vision, and (c) Priority Goals. These became the guiding principles for Wesley's strategic and operational plans for the next several years.

In addition, board members identified and approved a comprehensive list of guidelines for themselves. They assigned each of these to one of three categories—Skills, Goals, and Expectations. That list became the basis of board self-evaluation and was shared with new members during their fall orientation session.

The Chair

All boards need a skilled, dedicated chairperson. Wesley was blessed with a series of the finest: Wayne Smithey, Helen Smith, Isham Baker, and Ken Millian. I was pleased and proud to work closely with them. As each one approached the end of his or her four-year term, I worked with the board development committee in the selection of a successor.

The board adopted new bylaws which increased its effectiveness. One change allowed the retiring chair to serve one additional year on the executive committee, thus retaining his/her wisdom and experience for a longer time. Another innovation beefed up the level of expertise available to the board by allowing non-members with notable skills to serve on board committees, with voice and vote.

Faculty Selection

The issue of faculty selection came under discussion during the board/faculty retreats. The board already had the duty of giving final approval to all selections and promotions. It came to light, however, that many board members felt unable to cast an informed vote because they had not been adequately informed regarding the qualifications of the candidates. The board committee on academic affairs therefore adopted procedures whereby it could be involved in the selection and promotion process from the very outset—approving the position description and then reviewing the résumés of candidates to be interviewed. Further, board members would receive a résumé of the candidate as well as relevant comments from the search committee before they had to cast the final vote on the candidate.

American University

Given Wesley's close ties with The American University, Wesley's board thought it should establish a closer relationship with AU's board. It was therefore agreed that the president of each school would serve on the other school's board. Thus I served on the AU board for 10 years, beginning in 1992. I became acquainted with the senior officers of the university and interacted with them periodically around issues of common concern. They were always gracious and helpful. I believe the time spent there was worthwhile in maintaining a positive relationship between the university and the seminary.

When Ben Ladner became president of AU in 1994, he and I met a couple of times a year to share perspectives about the two institutions. He attended most of the Wesley board meetings and served on one very critical committee during Wesley's presidential transition.

Affirmative Action

Wesley Seminary had invested heavily in affirmative action since that racism workshop in the spring of 1983. After the Roy Morrison blow-up, board chair Wayne Smithey appointed the first affirmative action committee, which launched the seminary's vigorous investment in affirmative action. After a long period of work, the seminary's first affirmative action policy was written and approved in 1987. The affirmative action committee monitored all aspects of the work of the seminary and the AA officer made an annual report to the board.

In May of 1991, the board initiated an in-depth review of what had been achieved. As a United Methodist seminary, Wesley had already received a commendable review from the United Methodist Commission on Religion and Race. During the board meeting of May, 1992, Professor James Shopshire, the AA officer, presented the committee's report. The in-depth review went as far back as before the seminary moved to Washington, and forward to an examination of the existing affirmative action policy. It covered the seminary's hiring practices, along with the ethnic makeup of the student body, faculty, staff, administration, and board. It considered the positions held by minorities, along with comparative levels of compensation. They also examined Wesley's strategic plans and goals—and more.

My responsibility was to appoint the affirmative action officer and the committee and to support their work. The

181

AA officer did not report to me but to the board of governors. We worked closely together to move Wesley forward in the affirmative action arena. I kept the AA committee informed on all hiring processes and responded to any pertinent issues arising in the seminary.

While our affirmative action policy required commitment and persistence over a long time, it paid off. We became an increasingly diverse and, I believe, a more just community.

VI. Finance and Investments

<u>Risky Business</u>

Dark clouds had been gathering during the fiscal year 1990-91. The very next year, sunlight broke through in the form of a dramatic increase in enrollment. Suddenly we could see a $300,000 pot of gold at the end of a beautiful rainbow.

Enrollment continued to rise for the next four years, but the number of tuition hours did not. While new foundation grants helped fill our income gap, they did not resolve all of our fiscal issues.

We needed to launch a capital campaign to increase the seminary's endowment. For that, we would need to hire a consultant, pay for special events, and make long-term commitments to new staff. We also had other capital demands such as critical facilities improvements and a new computer system. On top of all that, we had increased everyday expenses. What we did not have was the means to pay for all those things.

After considerable thought and discussion, we decided to take a serious financial risk that made some of our board members uncomfortable. We set in motion a plan that would draw 10 percent from Wesley's endowment every year—3 percent for the long term development program and 7 percent for the operating fund. Our investments were producing an annual return of 12 percent, but it was not wise to let ourselves be seduced into thinking that would go on forever. We simply did not have a good alternative.

We were betting that our capital campaign would increase the endowment quickly enough to make our increased endowment draw more profitable than withdrawing a smaller percentage annually. Our needs were that pressing. The financial risk seemed reasonable.

The facilities budget posed another problem. Before I arrived at Wesley, the plant fund had often borrowed from the endowment to cover its expenses. But we were able to repay that debt during the 1980s. In the 1990s, our increased revenue actually produced a moderate surplus in the operating budget, which we transferred to the plant fund. (That meant the operating budget was always in balance but its surplus was never large.) In our big year of 1991-92, we were able to transfer $160,000 from the operating account to cover the cost of a new computer system. In addition, we assigned all undesignated bequests into the plant fund. In spite of all of these moves, money was draining out of the plant fund faster than we could put it in. Before very long, the plant budget was again running a deficit.

The Good News

Our bet had begun to pay off. By June 30, 1995, Wesley's financial situation had improved significantly. During the previous four years we had invested in new programs and staff, produced an annual surplus in the operating fund (transferred to facilities), built a capacity for a long term development program, and increased our endowment. Our newly-established seminary charitable foundation had more than $3 million in assets. That, plus an endowment of some $8.5 million, raised our total of invested assets above $11 million.

Members of the faculty and the board frequently asked how Wesley compared with other seminaries, United Methodist ones in particular. The Board of Higher Education and Ministry of the UMC answered the question in the fall of 1992. They sent out comparative data about the 13 UM seminaries, which shed interesting light on Wesley's position.

We had the third-highest number of students—547— behind Candler's 660 and Duke's 568. We had the largest number of UM ethnic students with 80. Our tuition was within $1,000 of all the other schools. Our institutional cost per student per year—$13,505—was the second lowest. Regarding faculty salaries, Wesley's full professors were third from the bottom, but their median level was fourth from the top. Our highest administrative salary came in third from the bottom, but the median for all administrative salaries came out on top.

In the last decade and a half, Wesley Seminary had made significant strides in strengthening its financial situation, but it was still undercapitalized. In our next phase we would address that issue in a more dramatic and successful fashion.

VII. Development

Will the Annual Fund Save Us?

I had not been at Wesley very long before it became apparent that raising money every year was deemed the critical need and the financial salvation for the seminary's future. Until we found prospects and asked for their support, nothing was going to happen. We worked hard at that and were dramatically successful in the beginning. By the end of my first year, the annual fund had been increased by 60 percent. In the second year it was up by 29 percent. I was surprised and delighted.

Having made a private assumption that such success would continue, I was not quite so delighted when from 1985 to 1990, annual fund increases settled into the range of single digits. Even when we broke the half-million mark in 1990, that represented only 14% of the seminary's total income. During the first half of the 90s decade, the annual fund's growth slowed even further. We were learning the hard way that our financial strategy had to be more than annual fundraising.

On the positive side, we also learned that regardless of the size of the gift, the givers developed an attachment to the seminary—a feeling of ownership. They became the most loyal and interested sector of our constituency. By word of mouth, they became advocates for Wesley within their churches. They came to seminary events and brought others with them. With some encouragement, they increased the amount of their gifts and later became our best prospects in a capital campaign. Many of them included Wesley in their estate plans as well. It became apparent to me that encouraging donors to make an annual gift generated overtones of support far beyond the sum of their gifts. Our success should not be measured by total dollars alone.

Our main development task was discovering, encouraging, and inviting individuals to become a part of the Wesley community. Cultivation occurred by a variety of means. Having individuals come to our campus and learn about the seminary and its mission enhanced the possibility they would become financial supporters. Thousands of people drove by the Wesley campus on Massachusetts Avenue daily. Very few knew about the seminary and its work. Numerous individuals, once on the campus, became attracted to its mission and captivated by its campus and personnel. Our task became one of providing opportunities for discovery. If they took the next step of making an annual gift, it provided the glue that made them stick with Wesley.

One of our most interesting and successful "get acquainted" programs was suggested by Ken Starr, a Wesley board member. He was then serving as the solicitor general of the United States and later special prosecutor. He and Charles Manatt, also a Wesley board member, who was the former chair of the Democratic National Committee, agreed to serve as co-chairs. Although they were unlikely co-chairs—political foes but Wesley colleagues—they had a shared enthusiasm for the seminary. They wanted to provide an opportunity for professional leaders in Washington to participate in substantive discussions and learn about the resources of a theological school. The group met once a month for breakfast and an hour of input by seminary personnel, followed by group interaction. This "Society of Community Builders" attracted 30 to 40 people every meeting and continued for over a decade. It was one of the places in Washington where Democrats and Republicans met for conversation and theological inquiry. In the process, Wesley provided a great service and expanded its constituency.

A New Source

The annual fund did not grow as much as I had hoped, but I discovered another source of financial support— foundations. I became aware that thousands of

186

foundations existed in America. They came in a variety of sizes and focus. We began to research them and make personal contacts. It soon dawned upon me that each foundation had its own distinctive set of preferences and was eager to establish relationships with others who were working toward similar goals. I was gratified to learn that some of them were open to supporting seminaries. I also learned that all of them had a legal (IRS) requirement to give away no less than 5 percent of their assets every year.

My experience identifying and cultivating individual donors carried over to the foundations. It was just as useless to mail an unsolicited proposal to a foundation as it had proven to be the case with individuals. Most of the foundations were managed by professional staff, and there was no substitute for personal contact with them. Once we got to know each other, the free exchange of ideas then produced mutually satisfying results. They paid careful attention to demonstrations of how Wesley would use their funds in a fashion that met their guidelines.

The seminary received its first significant foundation grant money, $66,250, in 1987. That increased to an average of more than $250,000 every year from 1990-1995, from a baker's dozen of our "friendly foundations." The powerful leverage of those efforts could not be ignored. Even a small grant provided the seminary with considerably more income than several generous individuals would muster, and grants quite often extended for several years.

Capital Campaign

In the spring of 1991, we launched a capital campaign to raise $10 million in two years. A year and a half later, we had raised only half that amount, virtually all of it from individual gifts and pledges. I thought we might have bitten off more than we could chew. Ideally, we wanted cash to put into the endowment fund so it could produce immediate income. That was not realistic, however; our donor base was not large enough for that. We needed a different strategy—namely, long-term deferred gifts.

The newly-created Wesley Charitable Foundation made it possible for individuals to invest in long-term gifts such as charitable trusts, annuities, etc. That was well and good, but we were able to take a further step suggested by one of our advisors. We created a "charitable gift bond" that would have the features of a charitable trust but without an income flow back to the investor. The donor would make a gift of, say, $15,000. The seminary would name that as a scholarship and put it into a long-term investment. Twenty years later, the bond would have matured into $100,000. That amount would then be transferred to the active endowment, where it would produce income for student scholarships. Ultimately, $4 million of our campaign total came from charitable gift bonds.

Our gift bonds had some downsides. First, the seminary had to be willing to tie up the money with no chance to use it until the bond reached maturity. Second, it would take a steady growth rate of 10 percent to produce $100,000 over the 20-year life of the bond. That was too optimistic. When the bull market broke around 2000, investments not only lost value, their growth rate fell off a cliff. The model would work only if we were willing to employ a very long investment strategy and a "no-spend-until-maturity" discipline.

We had made some earlier decisions that paid off in the campaign. Doug Cooney had been shifted from planned giving to campaign solicitation, Randy Casey-Rutland was hired as director of planned giving, and Richard Bailey was brought in as an estate-planning consultant. Through their efforts in concert with the entire development staff, the executive vice president, and the president, we generated over $5 million in 1993 and pushed the campaign well beyond the goal I had thought we couldn't meet. We recorded $10,351,664 in gifts from 151 donors. Sixty percent were endowment future gifts—charitable annuities, trusts, charitable gift bonds. Forty percent came in the form of cash gifts and bequests.

Disappointment

In December, 1992 I received a $65,000 check from the Denit Trust. A phone call to the investment manager of the Trust revealed an exciting prospect. Someone named Helen Denit had died and left a trust. Before her death she had informed one of the trust officers that she had three main interests, one of which was Wesley Seminary. She had been a member of a United Methodist congregation, although not very active. None of us had ever heard of her or the trust.

Unfortunately, Helen Denit had never put her wishes in a will or even a letter to the trust management firm. They had only that one officer's conversations with her. Now they were exploring the three charities she mentioned, seeking proposals as to how they would use the money. Much of the estate was tied up in a very valuable piece of land in the Washington area. The land would be sold and invested. It was projected to produce some $200-$400,000 annually for each of the three charities. In the meantime, the trust officers wanted to begin a relationship, provide some funds, and work with us to develop a larger and more permanent program.

Our excitement grew as we worked on our proposal. We communicated in person regularly with the trust officer; he even visited our campus. Our plan was to create a special scholarship program for selected students who would be named Denit Fellows. Wesley would contribute some of the funding, but the major portion would come annually from the Denit Trust. The trust officer liked the idea of honoring Helen Denit in this fashion. He encouraged us to announce the scholarship, begin slowly, and increase the number of fellows as more funding became available.

Alas! The Investment Management Company thought they could generate a greater return by developing the land themselves rather than selling it and investing the proceeds in the stock market. They were wrong. As a securities investment firm with little experience in developing real estate, they wasted several years and ultimately failed. A great percentage of the money was tied up and no longer available for distribution to the charities.

Because Helen Denit's wishes were never put in writing, we were at the mercy of the officers of the Denit Trust. They were totally free to decide where the money would go. We later learned that the Trust had made a gift of $1 million to the Heart Association of Baltimore, where one of the trust officers served on the board. We could not find out where all the estate money was going, but Wesley received only modest amounts. We had already set up the Denit Scholarship program, announced it, and put money into it. We continued to receive modest grants from the Trust, but we lost out on millions.

I must confess I found it difficult to "trust" trust officers after that experience.

<u>Lessons Learned</u>

Few schools have one dominant income source such as a large endowment or total funding from their sponsoring church or wealthy donors to cover year-end shortfalls. For most schools—certainly including Wesley Seminary—a balance of income sources had to be the answer. Over the 20 years of my presidency I learned that even in the fundraising portion of the seminary's income, a balanced approach was needed. I was disappointed with our annual fund production, but I came to understand its basic contribution to building a constituency and long-term development. Endowment building is a slow-growth enterprise which demands (a) the commitment and discipline necessary to generate long-term gifts, (b) a wise investment strategy, and (c) a policy of judicious spending. Foundations can be a significant income source only if a seminary tends this resource on a regular basis with the continual involvement of the seminary's top officials—not the least of which must be the president.

What does not work is fanciful thinking, hoping for that big gift that solves all money problems. Development must be continuous, relational, and creative.

VIII. Academic Programs and Faculty

The first half of the 1990s was a time of change that brought Wesley ever closer to its stated vision of becoming a church-based seminary. It was a time of exciting new programs and a commitment to a younger and more diverse faculty.

<u>Globalization</u>

Most of the faculty and administration, along with some board members, participated in cross-cultural immersions. Three of these were international and one was local. The local immersion actually took place in two locations—Applachia and the inner-city of Washington, DC. This heightened awareness of global issues spawned new programs and actions such as the protesting of apartheid in South Africa, a scholarship fund for African students, international degree programs, and a fresh Korean initiative. We added a cross-cultural immersion requirement to the MDiv curriculum. Each faculty member wrote a paper on the implication of globalization for his/her academic discipline. Several members engaged in international projects, many contributing their time to teaching in another cultural setting. The seminary's decade of investment in globalization had begun to bear fruit.

Changes in the MDiv

The Ministry 2000 project accentuated our relationships with local churches and annual conferences. We also organized covenant discipleship groups based on John Wesley's concepts of discipleship. Once a week for a year, each student and faculty member participated in a covenant discipleship group sharing his or her personal goals for growth and ministry. These sessions fostered personal commitment to individual ministry goals and accountability to the group for attaining them.

In accordance with our desire to strengthen ties with congregations, we re-designed field education and gave it a new title: The Practice of Ministry and Mission— PM&M. Each MDiv student would work within a congregation for two years, including forming a covenant discipleship group of laity. Wesley thereby embraced a large number of partner churches by making them, in effect, part of its extended campus. We had intentions of expanding the concept to include lay education and continuing education for clergy. That later evolved into the Wesley Ministry Network, which provided material for congregational education.

We also reached out to bring the church closer to the seminary by means of a pastor-in-residence program. Each semester, an active pastor would spend half time on campus. These pastors not only engaged with students, they sat in with PM&M groups, attended official faculty meetings, attended chapel, and had informal conversations with members of the faculty.

Urban Ministry

Out of Wesley's traditional commitment to urban ministry we developed a special urban ministry track in the MDiv program during the 1980s. We included a beefed-up version of that in the newly-formulated program in the 1990s. Eventually, we would establish a downtown center with student residences and classroom space.

In the early 90s, we worked with the Council of United Methodist Bishops to create models for urban ministries. Then we hosted a national symposium on urban ministry for each of the three years beginning in September of 1990. Our involvement in those endeavors included providing space, faculty, and logistical support, which included raising funds to help representatives of other seminaries and annual conferences to attend.

Expansion of the Doctor of Ministry Program

We overhauled the DMin to accommodate pastors who wanted to enhance their skills. First, we changed the class format and the location of classes. All courses became week-long intensives, with a block of them offered twice a year on the Wesley campus. That allowed a pastor to complete two of the required 10 courses in the span of two weeks. We offered the same intensives off-campus, usually in cooperation with a sponsoring church agency. Two courses could also be taken online or through another educational institution.

In response to requests from some annual conferences, we began offering specialty tracks within the doctoral program. The Virginia Conference, for example, wanted to develop a group focused on evangelism. The Tennessee conference wanted to offer Wesley Studies. As we added those and other specialty tracks, we soon noticed that several of them had taken root and were attracting pastors in increasing numbers—Pastoral Leadership, The Arts, Worship and Preaching, and Pastoral Care, to name a few. Enrollment swelled to the point that by 1995 we had more than 100 pastors in our DMin program.

We encountered some initial faculty resistance to teaching in the restructured program. Most of them, having no experience teaching those who were already practicing ministers, felt challenged to understand the pastoral environment. It was a radical change in several ways and would be an extra workload to boot. We offered an additional stipend for teaching in the DMin Those who dipped their toes in first, quickly took to the water and became advocates for the program. They became co-learners with the pastors. Those relationships ultimately influenced their methods of preparation and teaching of MDiv courses. Without a doubt, the revised DMin program brought new energies and new students to the seminary and moved us closer to our goal of becoming a church-based seminary.

XI. Center for Religion and the Arts

In fewer than 15 years, the Center for the Arts and Religion had taken root and flourished. The Wesley

194

community had embraced its mission and philosophy so warmly as to make the arts an integral part of the pastoral education experience. Furthermore, a modest endowment assured the Center's continued presence. All of that did not happen easily.

The Center's unique role in the seminary's life and educational program, its visibility both in and outside of theological education, and its unmistakable presence on campus made it the envy of many schools. Cathy Kapikian, the Center's founding director, was in great demand as a speaker and consultant in churches and seminaries. Several of them tried to recruit her for their own faculty. Many seminaries sought our advice on how to create such a center and its unique program.

My counsel to many presidents who asked to do it: First, find or support an already present creative genius to lead the charge. Next, listen carefully, observe, and risk the chaos that is implicit in introducing new meaning and modalities necessary for such a program. Cathy convinced me of the importance of the imagination and in particular the role of sight in proclamation of the Word. Our very visible studio with its open door policy housed an ongoing stream of resident artists whose painting, sculpting, hammering, burnishing, etc., made works mysteriously materialize. Cathy never wavered from saying, "Doug, this is a conceptually correct idea."

It was difficult for me to communicate succinctly what and how such an undertaking could happen at other schools. I never felt successful, often ambivalent, and sometimes haughty trying to express it. Yet I believed in our concept of how the arts could serve our mission, and that belief was reinforced time after time by the works of the artists and their impact on our students.

How did we make it happen at Wesley Seminary?

Two very different but essential ingredients came together: Cathy's commitment to the creative process and my commitment to the institution. She believed that theological education was incomplete without attention given to the creative process embodied in the arts. The arts provided a different way of learning, creating, and leading that opened an individual's imagination, insight, and leadership capacity.

I became convinced of the wisdom and power of her vision for the seminary. I also knew that dozens of "great new ideas" came across my desk regularly. Practically every faculty member had a pet theory about theological education. Our church constituency had its own ideas about good pastors and how to produce them. Almost every "new idea," regardless of its origin, required resources and change on the seminary's part. My responsibility was to keep the seminary balanced— focused on its mission and to generate the resources to support it.

Suddenly I was faced with this great new vision about the arts as an integral and practicing part of the seminary. Yes, it would require resources. Cathy never gave that a moment of thought. She was convinced that a right idea, if given a chance, would generate support both financial and from colleagues. In the beginning there was little room in the seminary's budget to expand any program. To legitimate the program institutionally I had to find a way to support it. Second, I had to clearly advocate for it and in some cases provide cover for it.

Not all of the faculty supported this new venture. Some of its critics would murmur, "What do the arts have to do with theological education?" Especially, we should not divert any dollars from the "essential" educational program to support the arts. The board also needed convincing. Over time, however, one creative initiative after another generated a positive cultural change. Slowly but surely, skeptics fell away, and the arts became an integral part of the seminary's life and mission. No other seminary has duplicated Wesley's program in religion and the arts, although Cathy always said we were building a prototype.

My Strategy

I put on my development hat. We needed to raise some new money for the arts so they were not seen as competitive with our other educational programs. I also knew that to give the arts a long-term, secure life at the seminary, we had to build a program and a support base that would sustain the arts long after Cathy and I were gone. We had to hedge against a future pharaoh that might not know Joseph, the artist, and thus diminish the program.

My first suggestion to Cathy was that we institute a Center for the Arts and Religion. I shared that thought with the board of governors in the spring of 1983. They approved it unanimously, though none of us knew exactly where it would take us. My notion was to create an advisory board, which would contribute ideas but ultimately become a fundraising arm for the Center. That proved to be less than successful.

Cathy was never keen about a board but she acquiesced and did her part, sharing ideas with the board and trying to encourage their ownership of the program. Several members of the board thought it should have governing authority over the Center, such as approving programs and budgets. I knew that was unworkable. Other members merely wanted to be associated with a creative arts program. I encouraged the members to support the Center financially and to introduce us to others with interest and financial resources. Even though I invested considerable time recruiting and working with the board, the members gave only modest annual gifts. It never became the successful development enterprise I had hoped for.

The Dadian Gallery

One advisory board member, a longtime friend of Cathy's, did produce in development. She introduced Mr. and Mrs. Arthur Dadian to Cathy and the Center. Cathy took them on a tour of the campus and the art facilities and shared the vision of the program, including the concept of a gallery unique to our mission. She captivated the Dadians. They pledged a gift of $100,000 to build a gallery at Wesley. The timing was perfect because we were in the midst of planning the renovation of the Kresge Academic center. We promised that a "Dadian Gallery" would have a center spot in the newly renovated Kresge.

The Dadian Gallery became a jewel on the Wesley campus. Our first gallery curator, Marvin Lieberman, had grandiose visions. He and Cathy aimed high, designing the gallery to museum standards in preparation for its place as one of DC's galleries. While the early exhibitions garnered critical acclaim in the DC media, it became clear that keeping its defining mission of exhibiting works at the intersection of art and religion, art and faith, creative processing and spiritual formation, became a stretch for Marvin.

One of Marvin's early shows, related to the aids crisis, displayed, front and center, a large painting of a nude male—with every part fully exposed. The opening was to coincide with a meeting of the Wesley Women's Guild—

198

not the most artistic-minded and liberal-thinking group. Marvin gave me a pre-show tour. I hated to act like an ultra-conservative art critic, but upon seeing the painting, I said, "Marvin, that picture has to go!" After some protest and a lecture about great art, he complied. Ironically, many of the women in the guild became ardent supporters of the arts program and the gallery.

Another early show featured an artist whose work consisted of sculptures made from trash of the culture—old car parts, out-of-date typewriters, etc. A dozen or so pieces were exhibited on the seminary quad. Some members of the faculty were horrified. The students thought they were hilarious. I commented as little as possible. One Monday morning not long afterward I walked onto the quad only to discover a dozen pasteboard boxes in many shapes, created by a group of students over the weekend. They had given each piece the name of a faculty member or administrator. It was uncanny how each work evoked an aspect of its namesake. Mine was particularly tale-telling.

Quite a few members of the campus community were peering out of windows waiting to see my reaction. I pronounced the works as innovative, in the spirit of the arts, and extending the frontiers of creativity. I suggested that such creative art called for a juried show and a prize to be given to the winner. We formed a committee of judges who made a selection, and we rewarded the student creator some silly prize. Almost everyone had fun. That is, except Marvin. He thought it depreciated the original show and the artist. Before too long Marvin found employment at a museum more appropriate to his interests.

I knew Marvin did not fit at Wesley, but I was extremely grateful for his creative gifts, energy, and vision that he brought to the creation and launching of the Dadian Gallery. Cathy assumed a greater role in the gallery, located a new curator, and integrated the gallery more clearly into the Center's overall approach and program.

Fundraising for the Arts

David McAllister-Wilson and I disagreed on the best approach for generating funds for the arts. He felt that we should include the arts appeal as part of the seminary's regular annual fund. My concern was that the special appeal of the arts would get lost in the general appeal. It might increase the annual fund goal but produce relatively little new income. I persisted in making the arts a separate approach.

Cathy was a creative architect with a clear vision about the arts in theological education. A fund-raiser she was not. I would get frustrated with her, occasionally infuriated. She had dozens of contacts with people of wealth who were excited about the arts and admired what she was creating at Wesley Seminary. However, I could not persuade her to ask them for money or to introduce them to me. She was very hesitant to talk with people about money. That was my job, but I needed her participation.

Somewhat out of frustration and lack of progress in fundraising for the arts I decided to hire a creative and energetic woman, Margie Dean Gray, to serve as executive director of the Center and Cathy as program director. Margie Dean's primary task was to raise money for the Center. Cathy cooperated but was never enthusiastic about the new structure. We had a line item in the seminary's income budget designated for the arts. We had modest success but never raised enough to cover the amount we were spending annually on the Center. Two years later Margie Dean's family moved to Colorado.

Our first significant success came through the Henry Luce Foundation. Its president, John Cook, had been on the faculty at Yale Divinity School and helped start a program on religion and the arts. Its focus, however, was primarily academic. Cook was interested and encouraging of Wesley's program, though he was never fully enthusiastic about our focus on the creative process that oriented it in practical theology. However, through John Cook and his successor Michael Gilligan the Luce Foundation made a series of three grants to encourage and support the Center for Religion and the Arts at Wesley. Together they totaled $585,000. This infusion of grant money solidified the Center's budget and encouraged its expansion to include drama, music, poetry, and dance along with the visual arts. This expansion and our earlier curricular revisions helped us weave the creative process of the arts into the fabric of theological education.

These grants, however, did not solve the long-term support issue. We needed some endowment to guarantee the Center's future. Two individuals made that dream come true. A long-term supporter of the seminary, Paul Blackwood, had an interest in the arts and theological education. David McAllister-Wilson had periodically taught a Sunday School class at Mount Vernon UMC where Paul was a member. Through David, Paul became interested in Wesley. He came to many events on campus, and David and I visited him in his apartment. He left his estate to Wesley but did not specify exactly what it should support; he left that to David and me. We decided to place his million-dollar legacy as the beginning of a small endowment for the Center for Religion and the Arts at Wesley.

The next building block came from Henry Luce III—Hank to his friends. He and I came to know each other through serving together for several years on the board of A Christian Ministry in the National Parks. The board met twice a year. He and I would meet for lunch in New York or Washington when an occasion would arise. I knew Hank loved the arts. As president of the Luce Foundation for 30 years, he had directed a lot of funding in support of the arts. Having shared with him the Wesley Arts Center story, I invited him to the campus for a firsthand look. Cathy led him on a private tour of the campus, studio, and gallery. Her charm and her enthusiasm for the unique approach of the arts at Wesley made a believer out of him.

Hank was supportive of the grants made to the Center by the Luce Foundation. At the conclusion of one of the grants we had a celebration of the accomplishments and invited Hank to speak. He gave a very affirming speech about Wesley's Center for the Arts and Religion. A couple of years later he invited Cathy to attend a Luce-sponsored extravaganza for the arts at the Pierre Hotel in New York City. I insisted she go where she again rubbed elbows with the rich and famous of the art world. But no money was forthcoming.

A few months later, I had a chance to visit with Hank when he was in Washington. We talked about the arts and our long-term vision for the Center. I told him of my concern about securing its future. We needed a small, designated endowment.

"How much?" he asked.

I suggested $1.5 million to enhance what we already had. I also suggested that we would like to name the Center for him because of the enabling support the foundation had given and his deep love for the arts. He said to let him think about it.

After he returned to New York, Hank proposed that the Luce foundation make a grant of 1.7 million to the Wesley Center. The grant was made and the newly named Henry Luce III Center for the Arts and Religion finally had enough endowment to assure its future.

Leadership and Change: A President's Story

Phase IV

A Maturing Seminary

1995-2002

I. Where We Were in 1995

Defining Wesley's Reality

A few weeks in Cambridge in 1994 and a few weeks at the beach the following summer provided me with some important reflection time. I returned to Washington in 1995 full of energy and excited about shifting into high gear.

In order to lay the groundwork for the next phase of our journey, I engaged the entire Wesley community in a broad assessment of our position as of 1995. I believed everyone needed a clear understanding of the school's mission, its challenges, and the opportunities that lay before us.

We had much to celebrate, starting with new additions to an already excellent core faculty. We had successfully completed a $10 million capital campaign. The Ministry 2000 project had strengthened relationships with our denominational base. Our student body held steady above 600 for the first time in history and was more diverse than ever. The DMin enrollment had risen dramatically without an adverse effect on the MDiv program.

Naming Wesley's Issues

In some cases, our successes spawned challenge. Commitment to a diverse enrollment had increased to the point where the majority of students were part time. That ramped up pressure on the faculty for more flexible scheduling of classes and advisory time.

We faced other difficulties not of our own making. The denominations we served were losing members and churches, thus reducing the number of positions available for pastors. Finances were tight: MEF continued to decline as a percentage of the seminary's income. The Annual Fund was stagnant. The veritable explosion of technology demanded new investment. Student loans were piling up.

Shaping a Vision for Wesley

Facing those issues, Wesley would need to create a new strategic plan to guide it into the 21st century. That could only be accomplished as a community endeavor. The president's role, as I saw it, was to facilitate this effort and invest energy and leadership on the issues most likely to make that process successful.

We were going to need a sound financial plan to support the roadway, including a major fundraising campaign. Removal of obstacles along the path would necessitate key personnel changes.

Our educational facilities needed some major renovation and additions. The new wave of information technology would require a significant commitment of new funds. Our educational programs and enrollment efforts needed clarity and decisions that would not be easy to make.

I had a few other items on my personal agenda, such as major gifts, a Center for Pastoral Leadership, the Arts Council, continued board development, and foundations. The road ahead, even if seen clearly, would be a steep hill to climb. No matter. I was convinced that Wesley Seminary had taken its first step on the journey to a newer and brighter future than ever before. I was determined to give it my best shot.

II. Personnel

Jim Collins' loading the bus metaphor always made sense to me. I learned quickly that who was on the bus and who sat where were the most critical elements for success. But having bright and skillful people was not enough. Their skills and temperament had to fit the job they were chosen to do.

As the bus driver—to push the metaphor one more step—I continually had to assess what skills the institution needed and how to find individuals who could fill those seats. Loading the bus never worked perfectly. Sometimes I placed a very good person in a seat only to discover there was a better fit somewhere else. Many times an individual outgrew the seat, but no better place was available. In the cases where relocation could be made, other occupants often became jealous or resentful.

By 1995 the Wesley bus was loaded with many capable individuals, most of them in the right seats and performing to acceptable standards. I soon had to consider who would become the next dean. In my mind there was one obvious in-house candidate—Bruce Birch. He was a long-term member of the faculty, an outstanding Old Testament scholar, an excellent teacher, and he possessed a good understanding of the educational processes needed in a seminary.

In accordance with my standard pattern, I discussed the matter with members of the executive committee of the board and received their approval to conduct a search for a new dean. I then interviewed all members of the faculty to hear their perspectives on what attributes we wanted and how we should conduct the search. I indicated that we should search for external as well as internal candidates. Everyone agreed.

Several members of the faculty mentioned Bruce as an outstanding candidate. The search went well. Bruce was right for the deanship—clearly head and shoulders above any other candidate. Moreover, he wanted the job, and I wanted him in the job. After the interview processes, we met over lunch. I explained what we needed in a dean and expressed my firm confidence in him. He choked up for a moment, and then said, "You will not be disappointed." I never was. He became an excellent dean. I clearly had another right person in the right seat on the Wesley bus.

Principles and Practicality

I had mixed feelings about personnel searches. I believed in the principles of affirmative action. Properly followed, they offered protection for the institution. They required—and thus enabled—us to seek out good candidates of diverse backgrounds. Ethnicity, gender, and sexual preference were not merely to be included but sought out. We had a commitment to those principles and endeavored to follow them.

At times a uniquely qualified candidate with the right talent, energy, and commitment appeared as a gift. I must confess, in some cases, I made selections based on my knowledge and judgment of what the seminary needed in a key position. I brought individuals on board without an open, affirmative-action-guided search process. On these occasions I felt deeply the conflict between principles and pragmatism, but I made the final decision. Every one of those few cases brought extraordinary benefit to the seminary.

A Dilemma

By 1995 I had some personnel concerns. They revolved around individuals with whom I had worked closely and for whom I had great admiration. Three years earlier, we had expanded David McAllister-Wilson's duties. He was to oversee the administrative offices of the seminary while retaining responsibility for institutional advancement, which included admission/recruitment and fundraising. I felt uneasy almost from the beginning about this arrangement. It spread him too thinly and required oversight of operational management details, which was not necessarily his strength. I became concerned that our annual fundraising was not growing significantly. The bottom line—David's instincts were external and strategic not internal and operational.

Kyunglim Shin Lee's gifts were also external. Without it being in her job description, she had begun fostering a Korean constituency for Wesley. She was good with students and performed well as dean of community life, but her passion gravitated toward Korean and global issues. In 1995 we shifted her job description and title. As vice president for church relations and student development she still had a hand in student affairs, but we expanded her responsibility to include church relations. That was a part of our expanded Ministry 2000 project. The change was actually a first step in recognizing her true gifts and interests. It freed her to focus more on external affairs, while not entirely removing her from student issues. A later step under David's administration would name her vice president for international relations and focus her energies entirely on building those relationships for Wesley.

David and Kyunglim were exceptional individuals with great personal gifts. Both would make extraordinary contributions to Wesley Seminary and its mission. Both were my close and trusted colleagues. My next personnel decision upset both of them. Though I was convinced about my decision, their unhappy reactions stung.

<u>Another Vice President</u>

For over a decade I had felt dissatisfied with how we were handling internal administration and personnel. Originally it fell under the purview of the business manager. That did not work to complete satisfaction. The different occupants of that seat on the bus were either good with finance or capable internal administrators, but not both. Budget wise I never felt we could afford a full-time person in each area. There were continuing complaints and suggestions from the staff that we needed a personnel officer. I did not disagree, but I never acted on it because of financial constraints. We continued to gerrymander that administrative area. After Cora Pickney became my executive assistant, she picked up some of the personnel work, but never full time.

Amy Northcutt, a lawyer, originally from Oklahoma, was the chief executive officer of the Interstate Commerce Commission. She had also earned an MA in religious studies from the University of Chicago Divinity School and had an abiding interest in seminaries. She was dissatisfied with government work and shared those feelings with a pastor friend, Charles Parker. He encouraged her to have a conversation with Chip Aldridge at Wesley Seminary. Upon talking with Amy, Chip quickly suggested that she should meet the president of the seminary.

Amy and I connected immediately. After a couple of conversations I made the journey downtown to her office. There I made her an offer she could not refuse—

vice president for administration and personnel at Wesley Seminary.

The offer generated a mixed bag of reactions. I had checked with Ken Millian, the chair of the board, who responded enthusiastically. I later shared with the administrative council what I proposed to do. Their reception was a bit frosty and mixed. Judy Stanfield, the VP for finance affirmed it. Cora Pickney liked it since it would remove her responsibility for personnel work. The dean was neutral. Kyunglim was upset, saying it was a bad idea to create another vice-president position and that I would generate a lot of criticism from the Wesley community. She was correct about the faculty. They thought it was another expansion of the administration, especially adding another senior officer. The staff was very pleased with the appointment since it met a need they had cited for years.

David McAllister-Wilson said very little in the council meeting but came to me immediately afterward. He felt this personnel move was a slap in the face for him. Did it mean that I felt he had not been doing a good job of supervision of the operational managers in the seminary? What did this mean for his position? Was it a signal that he was to be eased out?

I strongly assured him that it was not a reflection on his performance, but I had something more important for him to do. "What is that?" he asked immediately.

I reminded him that he and I had been assessing Wesley's current situation and what the seminary needed to do for the future. We had both agreed that Wesley had a major opportunity to go further in its mission to serve the church. It would mean taking a giant step in our relationship with the church and, in fact, commit the seminary to helping transform our constituent churches in the region. Such an effort would require a new strategic plan, a big investment of resources—personnel, program, and finances—and a major fundraising effort. I wanted David as my co-partner in leading this effort. He had the creative imagination, skills, and passion for such an effort.

When David left my office I was not sure either he or I grasped the full significance of what I was proposing. I do know that moment was the pad from which we would launch the next seven years' work. It would challenge the Wesley community, our constituency, and both of us. But it would elevate Wesley to a whole new mission and quality as a seminary.

As I look back, I believe that moment was also the first step in the preparation and affirmation of David McAllister-Wilson as the next president of Wesley Seminary.

I named Amy as our vice president of administration without an open search. That was my choice and my decision alone. She brought a new level of background, competency, and energy to the seminary. She successfully worked through a number of issues and staid administrative structures that helped renew our internal administration. With a cheerful presence, a positive attitude, and an affirming touch for those she worked with she helped transform the internal administration of the seminary. Her five years in the position were a gift to the seminary and to its president. With all our regrets but deep gratitude she moved on to become the deputy general counsel at the National Science Foundation.

Personnel Learning

Reflecting on Amy's avenue into the seminary reminded me of another very important personnel role in institutions. Chip Aldridge, the director of admissions, had recommended that Amy should talk with me. Earlier he had also suggested that I talk with Kyunglim Shin Lee when I was looking for a dean of community life. Chip was an important connecting link in the seminary and for me on numerous occasions. He even gave me feedback on one of my early sermons in the Wesley chapel. He came as a student just as I arrived as president and had continued to work in various positions following his graduation. He loved Wesley. His insight into the seminary community, its mission, and the attributes best suited for the Wesley bus enabled him to serve as an important linking role. I learned to listen and understand from Chip and others like him.

Raymond Washington was one of those "others" like Chip. At that time Raymond was working as manager of the mailroom and copy center—a central hub in the life and work of the seminary. An African-American, he started as a teenager working on the grounds crew. His energy, his integrity, and his love for the seminary enabled him ultimately to move into a key administrative job. He knew everybody at Wesley. His positive personality and presence made him a vital ingredient in the community glue that held the school together. He, Chip, and others like them, taught me a lot about the essential, internal ingredients necessary for effective institutions.

Other Appointments

Randy Casey-Rutland was serving in the development office as Director of Endowment Giving. As David McAllister-Wilson assumed more responsibility in planning and the capital campaign we named Randy as chief development officer. Later when Randy moved to Florida and Kathleen Hutchins retired as director of the annual fund, we chose Jane Deland, a Wesley graduate and a member of the board of governors, as director of development. She was a gifted and dedicated person and brought excellent leadership. She proved to be an important asset during our major campaign effort. David continued through all the changes to retain oversight of the institutional advancement work of the seminary.

In 1995 we had the opportunity to hire another Korean, Sam Lee, who had a doctorate in pastoral counseling, to serve as associate dean for student affairs and teach half time in the pastoral care area. He subsequently moved into full-time teaching, and we recruited Estrelda Alexander, an African-American, as associate dean of community life. She also served on the Administrative Council.

For two years, an excellent Old Testament professor, Denise Hopkins, coordinated the DMin program on a part-time basis. The program was growing rapidly, and we needed someone to give full attention to its development and management. Lew Parks fit the bill perfectly. He had significant experience as a United Methodist pastor and district superintendent. Lew stepped into the position of associate dean for church leadership development and directed the DMin As part of our strategic plan, he also led our efforts to provide educational resources and training in our four partner United Methodist annual conferences.

President's Office Support Staff

Another personnel challenge involved the support staff in the president's office. Executive assistant Cora Pickney and secretary Joyce Emmerling who had worked with me for seven years. Cora had the opportunity to move to the practice of ministry and mission office as assistant director. She wanted a new challenge, and I thought it was time for change in my office. Joyce then moved to the associate dean's office to manage housing and help Sam Lee with student affairs.

Those changes, as positive as they were, left me with the daunting task of finding a new support staff. Amy Northcutt assumed most of Cora's administrative work, but I still needed a special person to manage the office— and me. That called for someone with a passion for the church and the seminary, someone who could meet and greet a great stream of differing personalities. That unique individual turned out to be Mary Bates Washington. Mary was then serving as executive assistant to Wallace Charles Smith, pastor of Shiloh Baptist Church, a historic African-American congregation in Washington. One of the Wesley Board members, Benny Thayer, suggested that I do everything possible to recruit Mary. It took several meetings with her as well as considerable urging from Benny to convince her to say yes. I also thanked Wallace Charles for his support— reluctant though it was—in Mary's decision to accept the job.

Neither Mary Bates nor I realized the powerful effect she would have, not only on my work but on the entire Wesley community. She became our earth mother. She became a reliable and supportive partner for my final years at Wesley and has remained so even into my retirement years.

I did my office correspondence through a portable dictating machine. Mary would type and correct the messages for my signature. On her first day in the office I dictated my first message to her. To my surprise she

216

saved it for years and presented me a copy on the day I retired.

July 29, 1996
Hello, Mary Bates Washington.

This is the first tape you will receive from Doug Lewis, but I promise you there are many more to follow. I hope you will not find them too arduous, that you can understand me, and soon you'll begin to know my patterns of communication. Before I begin any dictation I want to say a personal word to you.

First, I'm very delighted that you're going to be a colleague with me and will help make me a better president, the president's office more effective, and Wesley Seminary a place of excellence.

Second, I need your help in so many ways I don't even know all of them. I need to depend on you for many, many things, especially how we communicate in and out of the office, written and verbal. I also need your head and your heart to think and to anticipate and finish the affairs of this office—your heart because of your commitment to ministry and your commitment to make us the best we can be.

Finally, I want you to be as open, honest, and candid with me as you possibly can. When you don't understand something, ask me. When you disagree, tell me. When you have suggestions, make them. I won't always agree with you in many decisions that I finally have to make, but I can make them best when I have the candid input as well as the care and support of my colleagues. That way we can be the most effective team possible.

Welcome, Mary Bates Washington.

Mary Bates took me seriously. She supported and facilitated my work and on many occasions gave me helpful suggestions and feedback. She was candid and direct. After hearing my first sermon in chapel, she responded out of her African-American Baptist background. "Doug, that was an excellent talk you gave this morning in chapel, but it wasn't preaching."

During those years we had a strong, effective, and diverse senior leadership team consisting of three white males, two white women, an Asian woman, and an African-American woman. Not only were we diverse in gender and ethnicity, but different in personalities, perspectives, and strong opinions. The loaded leadership bus cruised swiftly and effectively during my last phase at Wesley.

Our Humanity

Dealing with personnel has many interesting and sometime frustrating aspects for a leader. The most talented and competent individuals also have their personal likes, dislikes, quirks, peculiarities, and self-interests—as do presidents. These human characteristics manifested themselves in numerous ways. Fortunately, our leadership team had no vindictive personalities. All of us were committed to the success of the seminary, but each of us had self-interest and a desire for status and affirmation. I watched with interest as we decided each year how and where each person was listed in the community directory and the seminary catalogue. Who was listed under the president's office, the dean's office, or the institutional development office? The positioning reflected who reported to whom and the status they held in the community. A wrong placement, which happened occasionally, brought immediate protest from the individual.

A second and usually touchier issue was the matter of office space and its location. Logic often went out the window when self-interest came in the door. Who shall be located near the president's office? Who should be in the dean's suite? Who will be upstairs in the development office? Whose office will have more square feet?

In many cases I had to intervene, negotiate, and ultimately decide all these and other "humanity" issues— one of the "joys" of a president's office. I did my best to act non-judgmentally and with a sense of humor.

III. Vision and Strategic Plan

In my report to the board of governors in October of 1996, I nominated "Planning for 2001" as our primary task for the upcoming year. They agreed with my recommendation that we begin working on a strategic plan to guide Wesley Seminary into the 21st century. The board directed us to develop such a plan, including a financial plan, and present it to their May, 1997, meeting for approval.

Creation of that plan would be assigned to a representative committee that would consult widely with various parts of the seminary community both on and off the campus. The board, faculty, and administration would review the proposed goals and issues (including finances) during a retreat scheduled for February of 1997. In May, the finalized plan would be submitted to the board for approval.

David McAllister-Wilson and I served as coordinators of the planning process. David produced most of the drafts, which we continuously reshaped and revised. I felt like the starter at the Indianapolis 500 shouting, "Start your engines!" The year did feel like a race with many participants giving their best. The process seemed to build momentum from the sheer number of people aware of it and taking part in it—owning it.

A Historic Moment

As this period of inquiry and design progressed, a unique spirit began to emerge within our community. Thoughts about the future prompted reflections on the past. We became more acutely aware of what a valuable legacy we had inherited. Generations who came before us had built a small seminary in rural Maryland. They had supported it and given it a reputation for quality. In our time the seminary had grown into one of the largest of the United Methodist seminaries.

In the planning meetings with the faculty and board, and in conversations with churches, pastors, and bishops, we talked about Wesley's dynamic growth and progress as a theological school and its commitment to serve the church. We recounted how our enrollment had grown a whopping 66 percent since 1990. We had intentionally become a diverse community with a global commitment and mission. Our faculty had grown in size and quality. Through the Ministry 2000 project we had achieved a unique level of partnership with the four surrounding annual conferences of the United Methodist Church. Our finances had improved dramatically, with balanced budgets and steady endowment growth. Our board of governors had matured in its support and governance of the seminary.

We dreamed of a bold move that would expand and deepen the seminary's mission—"A Revitalizing of the Church in our Region." We knew these churches were experiencing a crisis in the loss of members, money, and spirit. The future of the seminary depended on our investment in the needs of the church and its ministry for the 21st century. United Methodism was our primary base, but we also committed to work with other denominations represented in the seminary's student body.

Many blamed the decline of the church on a failure of leadership. Some believed it was a lack of spiritual clarity and depth in the church's leadership. Others thought it was the lack of adequate practical skills. At Wesley, we were convinced those two trains of thought must be linked. We committed ourselves to the spiritual and personal formation of our students as well as imparting the knowledge and skills necessary for effective ministerial leadership.

<u>Wesley's Strategic Plan</u>

The following is a summary of the plan.

I. Our Identity

> Wesley Seminary exists to serve the Church and its mission to the world. It serves as the academy of the church, preparing ministerial leadership for the Church.

II. Our Strategic Vision

Wesley will strive to create a learning environment in which the "church loves God with its whole mind" by pursuing faithful scholarship and striving for excellence in ministerial leadership. Wesley intends to accept and prepare for ministerial leadership only those men and women who show high potential to lead the church in mission and ministry in the world.

III. Our Strategic Goals and Issues

To realize this vision Wesley must make some fundamental advances in the next five years. This plan outlines our intention to focus our time and resources on a few key strategic issues and goals.

A. Strengthening our Relationship with the Church

Wesley will make more effective use of its academic resources by exploring new models for equipping the ministries of the church and encouraging the church to recommit to high standards in preparation of church leadership. Besides strengthening the seminary's curriculum, it will develop pilot models for lay education and clergy continuing education. Our vision as a theological school is to play a key role in the revitalization of the churches in our region.

B. Enlisting high quality candidates for ministry

By 2001, Wesley will have fewer total students who will be academically prepared, vocationally focused, with high potential for ministerial leadership.

To achieve that goal, Wesley will limit tuition hours to 8500, develop an effective feeder system within the church, and increase financial aid.

C. Forming Persons for Ministerial Leadership

Over the next five years Wesley, working with its church constituency, will devote more research, time, and resources to determine how best to form ministerial leaders for the 21st century. It will embrace its community of diversity within the unity in Jesus Christ in order to form persons for ministry in the world of diverse cultures of the 21st century.

IV. Strategic Budgeting: developing financial resources for educational excellence

Over the next five years Wesley will generate sufficient endowment, capital investments, and annual gift income to provide a quality faculty and educational environment, while keeping tuition costs affordable.

V. Institutional Advancement Campaign

Wesley will conduct a holistic campaign that will: (a) initiate a $20 million capital campaign, b) strengthen its relationship with the Ministry 2000 conferences, c) continue recruiting partner congregations and individuals, d) double the number of people making annual donations.

This strategic plan moved Wesley one step further toward focusing its mission on revitalizing the churches in its region. We no longer viewed the seminary as merely an academic institution but as an agent of change and renewal. That seemed presumptuous—and it was. Could a theological school seriously affect the life and ministry of the churches in its region? I remembered the 1989 board meeting when Clare Stanford, a lay member of the board, set a new course for the seminary with his dramatic question: "Does Wesley care about its relationship with the Church?"

Now we could clearly answer, "Yes, Clare, we do."

Successful or Not?

The question remained: what should be the relationship between a theological school and the Church? Wesley's mission shift—to invest in renewal of the churches in its region—was a bold and costly attempt to bring its denominational connections and their congregations into a closer relationship with the seminary. The purpose was to create a partnership around leadership development and effective ministry at the congregational level.

How successful was Wesley in bringing about renewal of the church in its region through investing directly in congregations and conferences? Speaking candidly, the impact was limited. There were countless illustrations of changes in some congregations and individuals, but little permanent organizational change in conferences and congregations in terms of how they conduct their ongoing ministries. Among our partner conferences and congregations, the project did foster a greater awareness of the seminary and its educational programs.

This major investment of time and resources affected the seminary's understanding of itself. It had an influence on many faculty members with respect to their methods of classroom instruction and their decisions about future programs. It moved us away from pure academics toward a deeper commitment to applied theology and effective practice. It went beyond mere technique into considerations of how to lead a congregation in the faithful pursuit of its mission in the 21st century. In practical terms, it helped in our recruitment of students and in fundraising from individuals and congregations. It confirmed our mission of preparing leadership for the Church and transforming the seminary into an up-to-date theological resource for the Church—and the world.

IV. Capital Campaign and Development

During the first 13 years of my tenure, the seminary had made significant progress financially. Now the time had come to make a giant leap toward increasing Wesley's capital base.

Individuals, foundations, and church groups gave money to the seminary because they believed in its mission. In the final analysis, however, fundraising was built on personal relationships between donors and the key members of the seminary. Their gifts were based on confidence in those individuals.

Longevity—the 13 years I had successfully served Wesley—was a significant asset, as well as my long-term partnership with David McAllister-Wilson. The positive influence of our stellar faculty and the increasing number of notable and effective board members were no less important. Our work, and that of generations who preceded us, had given Wesley a reputation for quality and reliability. Our extended support community of individuals and church leaders had grown from local to regional and now had become world-wide. I wanted the seminary to benefit from that reservoir of good will and admiration.

I was unsure how much we could raise. Our first capital campaign generated $5.2 million. The second one topped $10 million. Would $20 million now be possible? I knew that most fundraising campaigns depended primarily on a few large contributions. If that held true for us, we would need several gifts in the million-dollar range. During my first days at Wesley, I had wondered whether I knew anyone I could ask for $1,000 dollars. Was there now anyone I could ask to give a *million dollars?* Really? I confess to a few moments of doubt.

A Surprise Gift

Earlier in the campaign I had invited Mary Elizabeth Joyce, to my office for coffee and conversation. Although getting on in years, she was a most energetic and interesting person with whom to talk. She had been a regular but modest donor to Wesley, and was a dedicated church member. Setting her coffee cup down, she looked and me and said, "Dr. Lewis, what does Wesley Seminary really need?"

Somewhat surprised, I said, "Well, Mary Elizabeth, very few people ask me that directly. But I have always believed the heart and soul of a school is its faculty. What Wesley needs most is long-term support for its faculty. Endowing a faculty chair would be the most significant gift we could receive."

"How much would that cost?" she asked.

I told her: One million, two hundred and fifty thousand dollars.

She said, "Let's think about that," and prepared to leave. A week later she called and asked if she could come to my office. After some brief chit-chat, she said, "That idea of a chair; I would like to do that."

I almost fell out of my chair. Regaining my composure, I indicated how fantastic that would be for the seminary.

Mary Elizabeth had accumulated her money over a long period by making her own investments. She asked whether we preferred receiving payment in small-cap or large-cap stock. I blurted out that we would take any cap stock. She said it would take a few days to make arrangements, but I was not to worry—the seminary would receive the money.

After she left, everyone in the president's office and the development office danced a jig in honor of Mary Elizabeth Joyce. A million-dollar gift—without even asking for it!

A week later I received a letter itemizing the stocks that she proposed to transferred to Wesley. In conclusion, the letter said, the list would complete the $250 thousand gift. I was stunned. I read and re-read the letter. I called in Jane Deland, the director of development. Jane, who had been present during the conversation, confirmed the figure I had quoted.

That was a stunning moment. How could Mary Elizabeth have possibly misunderstood me? Even more stressful was the question of what to do next. After several anxious hours, I finally mustered up the courage to call her. She greeted me in her usual affirming way. I then said, "Mary Elizabeth, your endowment of a chair at Wesley Seminary is a marvelous gift. It will guarantee the support of a faculty member in perpetuity. I just wanted to thank you again for your gift of one million, two hundred and fifty thousand dollars."

A long pause ensued; I could hardly breathe. She finally said, "One million two hundred and fifty thousand dollars?"

I said, "Yes. That is how much it takes to support one faculty member."

Another pause ensued. Once again, I struggled for breath.

She said, "Well, I thought two hundred and fifty thousand was pretty cheap. But I'll do it anyway. It may take a little longer, but you will get the full amount."

I began to breathe again.

"Dr. Lewis."

"Yes?"

"May I give you some advice?"

"Absolutely."

"When you say one million dollars—*speak up.*"

Mary Elizabeth had more to give than money. She said, "Wesley Seminary performs a great service to the Church and the world. I am honored and grateful that I can be a small part of its ministry. Please allow others to have the opportunity to share in it." She then gave me a lesson in basic arithmetic by informing me that whereas a million might be a considerable amount, it has just three more zeroes than a Wesley Council gift of one thousand. I heard the message.

Not every gift fell into our laps like that one, of course. But every gift had its own story of personal interest, of generosity, and a belief in the mission of the seminary. In the campaign we received 10 gifts of a million dollars or more each—a reality that seemed almost unbelievable. Back in 1982, I would never have imagined in my wildest dreams that we would reach that level of affirmation and support.

During the next three years, the staff and the board, along with many individuals, churches, and other institutions, put forth a tremendous effort to complete the most successful capital campaign in Wesley's history.

We began with a goal of $20 million. Having reached that amount before the end of the campaign, we increased the goal to $28 million. By the end of the campaign we had raised $30.4 million. Amazing!

We began with the basics—planning, a case statement, goals, and organizational design and effort. But the success of all of those rested on the many relationships we had developed over the preceding years. My heart still beats a little faster when I remember the host of individuals who gave so generously. I can still picture those people whose care, love, and generosity changed Wesley Seminary and enriched my life forever.

<u>From Strategic Plan to the Capital Campaign</u>

The strategic plan, generated by a year and a half of groundwork, set the stage for the campaign. In the process we also developed a 10-year financial plan which was designed to cover the expenses of our current programs, facilities, and personnel, plus four new initiatives, which we summarized as follows:

Enlist a Generation of Leaders

We would invest in church-based enlistment efforts, add to our current scholarship budget, and designate $4 million for scholarship endowment.

Provide Excellence in Education

We would add four endowed faculty chairs, special funding for outreach programs, plant renovations, and increased annual funds.

Launch Bold Initiatives

We would extend programs and leadership development into congregations and annual conferences to enhance the education of leaders beyond their seminary experience. That would require additional staffing, upgrading our technological capacity, and building church partnership programs in ministerial leadership.

Gather a Generation of Partners

We wanted a dramatic increase in the number of people regularly involved with Wesley through a working network of local United Methodist conferences, a network of 200 partner congregations, 2,000 new supportive laypersons, and a stronger relationship with our graduates.

We estimated the cost of those four initiatives at $20 million over the next 10 years and set that as our goal of the campaign. We selected David McAllister-Wilson as director of the campaign. He would be supported by an elaborate organization of staff, board members, and volunteers. Each of the four initiatives would have its own committee with a chair.

Although I met with each of the committees on a regular basis, David did most of the coordination work. My work focused primarily on prospect identification, cultivation, and solicitation.

Board Approval

The board of governors approved the strategic plan in May of 1997. In October of that same year, we brought the capital campaign proposal to them for discussion and approval. Prior to the October meeting, Chairman Ken Millian sent a letter to all board members.

He began with a quote from Ecclesiastes 3:1:

> For everything there is a season, and a time
> for every matter under heaven.

He concluded:

> I believe this is the season for Wesley
> Seminary. I hope you will be present and
> fully participate in the dialogue and
> decision-making that will guide the
> seminary into the future.

After completion of his term as board chair in the spring of 1998, Ken graciously signed on as co-chair of the campaign steering committee. His leadership and the involvement of many members of the Wesley board proved integral to the success of the campaign.

Periodically, it would occur to me how critically important that group of board members was to the seminary. The governance of higher education institutions in America begins and ends with dedicated volunteers. Most of them were there not because of their expertise in academic subjects or educational methodology, but as the final governing authority of the institution. As fundraising became an increasing necessity for Wesley (and many other schools), it became a top priority to select board members with financial resources of their own—or those who could identify and influence others of means. They were not compensated for their investment of time and involvement in the affairs of the school. They did so because they believed in the school and what it stood for. The seminary relied heavily on that remarkable group. As president I speak for many others in my heartfelt thanks to every one of them.

The board's decision to approve the campaign proposal was a radical, downright risky move. It called for an expanded understanding of our mission—renewal of the Church—and, to be successful, a larger financial leap than ever before. The board of volunteers and their chosen president, along with his selected staff, were committing the seminary to sail into uncharted waters from which there could be no turning back.

It is unlikely that many board members viewed the situation as dramatically as I did. My senior staff and I had grappled with those ideas for two years. Secretly, I hoped my last hurrah was the right one for the seminary. I wanted everyone to be clear about our mission and willing to take the risk in pursuit of it. I wanted Wesley to be blessed with a strong and secure financial base to ensure its well-being far into the future.

The board approved our proposal by unanimous vote. Even further, individual members of that same board continued to give time and money during the next four years to help us become enormously successful.

Campaign Results

The final campaign report as presented to the board in October of 2001 showed a breakdown of the number of gifts as shown in the following chart:

| | | Original Estimate | | Gifts/Pledges Received |
Size	#	Amount	#	Amount
$3,000,000	1	$3,000,000	-	N/A
$2,000,000	1	$2,000,000	2	$4,800,000
$1,000,000	3	$3,000,000	8	$12,483,881
$750,000	4	$3,000,000	3	$2,621,806
$500,000	5	$2,500,000	2	$1,360,000
$250,000	6	$1,500,000	7	$2,648,659
$100,000	15	$1,500,000	17	$2,291,789
$50,000	20	$1,000,000	15	$970,622
$25,000	30	$750,000	36	$1,166,170
$10,000	50	$500,000	77	$1,087,122
$1-9,999		$1,250,000	-	$977,830
Totals		$20,000,000		$30,407,879

V. Striving to Become a Church-based Seminary

A Lilly Endowment Grant

While Wesley was developing its strategic plan and committing to a capital campaign to fund it, the Religion Division of Lilly Endowment was conceiving a new level of funding for theological schools. Its objective was to motivate the development of programs that could "Enhance Congregational Leadership." Lilly competitive

233

grants were generous and challenging. A seminary would need to engage cooperatively with its supporting churches to develop new models of preparing and supporting individuals to become effective parish pastors.

For Wesley, that was an exceptional opportunity because it aligned perfectly with our strategic plan. I spoke with the Lilly Endowment staff to ascertain their basic intent. We applied for one of the grants and received it—$1.5 million over a five-year period. Thinking through the grant proposal moved us to a better understanding of how we would work with our partner conferences and congregations on our common goal of improving the quality of ministerial leadership. The new funding enabled us to add additional staff, programs, and information technology to our efforts. We named the proposal:

Instituting a Church/Seminary Partnership to Improve the Quality of Ministerial Candidates

The proposal was structured in three stages which corresponded to existing patterns in a candidate's development: (I) a calling that moves one toward seminary; (II) discernment and preparation in seminary; and (III) establishing patterns and practices in ministry which will determine the long-term quality and effectiveness of a pastor's ministry.

I.   Creating a Culture of Call

In order to find a new generation of candidates, we proposed to re-institute a "Culture of the Call" within the Church. We sought to remind and assist the Church at key points where consciousness-raising about ministry took place for individuals, such as worship settings, youth groups, campus ministries,

234

special programs, etc. The four annual conferences encouraged all their congregations to have an annual ministry Sunday, during which the pastor would preach on his or her call to ministry. There would also be special programs and services for young people.

Our 200 seminary-partner congregations would make special efforts in this area. The seminary sent them specially-designed literature and videos about a call to ministry. Our faculty and staff preached in many congregations during their ministry Sundays. In each of these services we asked members to write the names of individuals they thought had potential for ordained ministry. We then sent a follow-up letter to each individual whose name was suggested. Most recipients were astounded to learn that other people saw potential for ministry in them. We invited them to special events at the seminary. During the next few years, dozens of those young people actually enrolled at Wesley to pursue their call to ministry.

II. Discernment and Preparation for Ministry.

We focused on three influence points during this stage:

A. Seminary Admissions and Evaluations

During the admission process, we spent more time counseling and advising students. We redesigned our financial aid structure to assist and encourage high-quality candidates. We held special events to help them explore their call to ministry.

B. Conference Committees on Ministry

We worked with conference committees on ministry, encouraging them to form advisory groups for those going through the discernment and candidate processes. The seminary provided materials and sometimes personal assistance in that endeavor.

C. Faculty and Pastor Mentors

On campus, we developed mentor pastors and faculty to work with students on discernment and evaluation of their calls during their seminary experience.

III. Establishment of Patterns for Effectiveness in Ministry

The United Methodist Church had just established a new three-year probationary period for individuals entering the conference and seeking ordination. Most conferences had an inadequate process for assisting young pastors to establish patterns of effective ministry during their early years. The seminary stepped up and offered help for this critical formative period. It included the training of supervising pastors, continuing educational events, and assisting conferences to develop special programs for young pastors.

All of these new seminary programs required a significant outlay of funds. This program support, funded from the foundation grant, moved the seminary ever closer in partnership with the participating conferences and congregations. The real payoff, however, was the number of young people who were influenced to enter ordained ministry.

A Seminary's Mission, Tradition, and Barriers

Wesley was pushing the boundaries of its mission. It had always claimed a close relationship with the United Methodist Church. Now understanding the seminary as *church-based* required a re-orientation of how we functioned as a part of the church and how we served it. The easy, traditional answer was that we prepared men and women for leadership in the church. That meant basically offering degree programs directed toward that end. Suddenly we announced that our deeper-level mission was to help bring about "renewal of the churches in our region." That was a whole new kettle of fish. No longer would we merely offer degree programs; we would now make direct interventions into the life and ministry of annual conferences and congregations.

Our latest strategic plan, the capital campaign, and then the Lilly grant refocused our efforts both inside and outside the seminary and its traditional programs. The board, faculty, and administration all said yes to this new thrust. None of us, however, grasped the full implications of such a move. We discovered many barriers in our path, tempting us to fall back to the old familiar programs.

We discovered the United Methodist annual conferences were using a rather unwieldy system for calling, preparing, and evaluating candidates for the ministry. Our proposal suggested unprecedented cooperation between the seminary and its four partner conferences. Ironically, the heavy demand for resources to implement the project would exceed our capacity. We therefore had to limit our participation in the very program that we had originated.

I think that the project, though it did not completely fulfill its lofty goals, had a positive effect on how the seminary and its partner churches perceived each other. Everyone understood that we shared the mission of preparing effective leaders for the Church and a commitment to the renewal of the churches in our region. Wesley would go forward, building on this new level of trust and understanding to produce further programs and resources dedicated to effective ministry in congregations and would rethink its educational programs for preparing people for ministry.

Habits of the Academy

Wesley had obstacles to face. Seminaries are constructed on the model of a university. It is all too easy to act as a self-contained entity that knows its mission—delivering academic courses, giving degrees, and doing academic research. With little operative contact between seminaries and churches, the faculty tends to measure quality internally, based on academic content instead of how the student will ultimately perform in the practice of ministry.

The seminary/church project did effect some positive change within our faculty members. Many of them taught courses and produced materials for congregations, pastors, and laity. The DMin program brought practicing pastors into face-to-face contact with faculty and forced the faculty to design learning processes that paid serious attention to the interests and perspectives of pastors.

Bridging theory and practice had been a long-term interest of mine. From my earliest days at Wesley I tried to keep this issue alive and working in everything the seminary did. The decade of the 1990s—its projects, plans, and grants—led the seminary more deeply into the struggle to become church-based. I believe we succeeded in the establishment of an interactive working relationship with our partner conferences and congregations toward the common goal of identifying, preparing, and sustaining individuals in effective ministerial leadership. That partnership also had a positive effect in the seminary and its educational programs.

VI. Board of Governors

I came to the seminary in 1982 with a firm belief that a successful educational institution must have a strong and effective governing board. If Wesley was to realize its full potential, the board and the institution would both have to undergo considerable change. Given the pressure of finances, most seminary presidents thought that financial capacity—giving and getting—ranked at the top of the list for board effectiveness. Without saying so, I shared that assumption. However, my two decades at Wesley and the transformation we went through gave me a deeper insight into the role of the board. I came to affirm four basic functions of the board:

A. Clarity and Affirmation of Mission

The evolution of Wesley's board did not take place quickly. Over the years, several factors contributed to its development: (1) recruiting capable and committed new members; (2) having to confront challenging institutional issues and make significant decisions; (3) engaging in ongoing strategic planning with faculty and administration; (4) continuing education for board members, including opportunities to engage with other seminary boards. The fruit of this development process produced a board that was clearly committed to the mission of Wesley Seminary. I was impressed by the decision-making process that was influenced by the board members' understanding of the seminary's mission. It became the guidepost for the work and measuring rod for their action.

The same thing happened to me. I came to realize to understand the seminary's mission and to affirm it was the foundation upon which all else rested.

I supported the board's growth by means of basic chores such as constantly searching for high-potential members, designing board meetings, providing informative material, planning retreats and educational events, and generating foundation support for member education.

B. Developing Policies

One of the board's most essential obligations was to establish goals and institute policies which reflect community values. Changing times often made this a difficult task. Over the years, the Wesley board grappled with hot topics such as affirmative action and sexual harassment. Each year, they reviewed their policies and revised them when necessary.

This core function also involved working with the administration to develop and oversee a long and ever-changing list of in-house policies such as personnel handbooks, employee benefits, investment policies, and budget guidelines.

C. Financial Responsibility

The board had fiduciary responsibility for Wesley. They reviewed the annual budget, approved it, then made sure the administration lived within its guidelines. (Should the seminary face bankruptcy, they would have to deal with the situation.)

One of the most significant shifts in higher education in the 20th century was the sharp decline of income from traditional sources. As a result, the pressure to make up the shortfalls fell to board members; they needed to "give more and get more." In 1982, there was simply not much "give" in the board's makeup. Gradually, through recruitment of new members and raising the consciousness of current members, the board increased its contributions markedly. By 1997 board members had become the source of 24 percent of Wesley's annual fund and further pledged a whopping 25 percent toward the upcoming capital campaign.

D. Selecting, Evaluating, and Supporting Presidential Leadership

The board provided a framework of mission clarity, policies, and finance. They then delegated operational responsibility to the chief executive—me. I was their agent and was accountable directly to them. I then selected senior staff to administer various areas of the seminary. The board retained approval power over job positions that I deemed necessary, but they did not vote on the individuals I chose to fill those slots.

They reviewed my performance every year. I served without a contract, entirely at the pleasure of the board. That was not a problem. From day one, the board had supported the various initiatives and programs that I proposed. As individuals and as a group they encouraged my continuing growth and supported numerous opportunities for my learning and renewal.

As part of its own growth and development, the board took action in 1995-96. It set up a committee to clarify its responsibilities. Under John Derrick's leadership, members reviewed their bylaws and policies. An excellent report summarized their findings.

At one point in its research, the committee ran across an obscure bylaw requiring annual re-election of the president. After having approved my work every year for 13 years, the committee members suddenly decided to vote whether I should or should not be retained for the upcoming year. They derived great pleasure from milking the situation for all its humorous value by announcing that I had been serving illegally for more than a decade. Then, graciously, they decided to ignore their past errors and recommend that I be re-elected for that year.

Chair of the Board

From the very outset of my tenure, I knew that chair of the board of governors was a critical position and that whoever held it could affect the well-being of the entire seminary. Although bylaws did not specify a term length for the chair, Wayne Smithey set a precedent. His term began on the same day I assumed the presidency. After four years in office, he declared that length of service seemed appropriate, and stepped down. Successive chairs followed his example, with two exceptions: Helen Smith's 12 years of board membership expired after she had served only three years as chair. Cliff Armour served a one-year interim term when Isham Baker had to delay his acceptance for a year after his election.

The board development committee held responsibility for proposing a slate of officers each year. As president, I had no formal authority to select board members or the chair. I did, however, have significant influence in those decisions and therefore played an active role in the committee's work. Shaping and developing the membership of the board and its officers in large part rested on my shoulders, and I was ever-mindful of that.

My pattern from the beginning had been to converse with the board chair at least weekly, in person or by phone. None of the chairs tried to control my actions. What each wanted was to be kept abreast of what I was thinking and planning—no surprises, please. That was a mutual desire; I wanted the board and the president always to be on the same page.

Each person who served as chair brought special gifts to the position. Wayne Smithey pushed me to think through issues thoroughly, top to bottom. Helen Smith exercised her influence to get the board to turn our brainstorms into reality. Isham Baker's very presence on numerous occasions embodied Wesley's commitment to diversity. He quietly pushed for justice on every front. Ken Millian, an excellent strategist and pragmatist, had a strong determination to get things accomplished. Robert Mallett had less time for the chair's role because of his high-level position in government, but he came through at the critical moment of presidential transition.

Twenty years on the job intensified my appreciation for the vital contribution that a board chair can make. Those who served during my tenure helped make me a better president and Wesley a better seminary. Each one shall always occupy a special place in my heart.

Makeup of the Board

By the Fall of 1996, the board had undergone dramatic change. Only one member remained from 1982—Helen Smith had agreed to return after a one-year absence.

The chart below shows the makeup and diversity of the board members, including the bishop of Washington and the president, who were both ex-officio.

243

Gender		Geographic Area	
Male	27	MD	11
Female	12	DC	12
		VA	11
Wesley Graduates	7	Other	5
Clergy Occupation		**Lay Occupation**	
Bishop	3	Business	17
Church Agency	2	Church Agency	1
Educ. Leader	1	Church Leader	2
Parish Minister	4	Civic Leader	1
Retired	1	Law	5
		Soc. Agency	2
Clergy Total	11	**Lay Total**	28
Ethnic Group		**Age Group**	
Asian Male	2	Under 45	2
Af. Am. Male	5	45-60	18
Af. Am. Female	3	Over 60	19
White Female	9		
White Male	19	**Denomination**	
Hispanic	1	UMC	34
		Other	5

VII. Enrollment, Programs, and Faculty

Enrollment Competition

In the highly competitive arena of education, student enrollment has a direct bearing on survival. Wesley had just set new records for enrollment during the 1990s when suddenly, in 1998, four new seminaries staked claims in Washington—three extension sites and one main campus. All of them offered graduate programs similar to Wesley's.

In spite of the seminary achieving a record 8,507 tuition hours in the 1997-98 school year, I was aware that enrollment numbers could be fickle. We were in the midst of implementing an ambitious strategic plan and straining to meet the goals of a 10-year financial projection. Tuition had been providing some 45 percent of our income, so any threat to that source had to be given serious attention.

Wesley did have an endowment, but that provided only 11 percent of our income and its growth had been modest. Moreover, our strategic plan called for building the endowment while reducing the draw against it, so we could not look to that source for budget relief in the foreseeable future.

Annual fundraising contributed about 15 percent of our income. We could, yes, attempt to raise more money every year, but experience had taught us to regard that as an iffy proposition at best. The United Methodist Church's MEF fund was also in a shrinking mode.

What to do? Try as I might to find an alternative, the figures running through my head always pointed to the same conclusion: enrollment had been and would continue to be the key to Wesley's economic well-being. During the 1980s, enrollment had crept slowly upward through the 300s, while tuition hours hovered in the mid-6,000 range except for two anomalous years.

Year	MDiv	MRE/MA	MTS	DMin	Others	Total	Tuition Hrs
1981-82	223	11	20	37	36	327	6228
1982-83	224	14	24	39	38	339	6300
1983-84	267	17	29	33	30	376	7578
1984-85	280	22	35	30	25	392	7682
1985-86	263	19	30	28	30	370	6770
1986-87	240	15	39	38	28	360	6408
1987-88	235	22	34	36	32	359	6436
1988-89	230	15	42	41	35	363	6383
1989-90	231	16	43	54	48	392	6496

In the first half of the 1990s, enrollment made a dramatic jump into the 500s. It kept growing and broke the 600 barrier. Tuition hours climbed into the upper 7000s.

Year	MDiv	MRE/MA	MTS	DMin	Others	Total	Tuition Hrs
1990-91	237	17	44	68	41	407	6740
1991-92	293	19	63	73	64	512	7800
1992-93	314	27	58	96	76	571	7909
1993-94	330	31	55	110	78	604	7780
1994-95	316	31	52	112	90	601	7785

The last half of the 1990s moved us into a steady average enrollment of 650 or above. Tuition hours passed 8000 before regressing slightly.

Year	MDiv	MRE/MA	MTS	DMin	Others	Total	Tuition Hrs
1995-96	365	18	57	155	56	651	8028
1996-97	338	15	65	168	86	672	8507
1997-98	320	7	61	187	93	668	8212
1998-99	301	8	63	182	51	605	7871
1999-00	305	20	63	139	87	614	7415
2000-01	311	25	77	148	85	646	7915

Our strategic plan had set a goal of 8,500 tuition hours. We hoped to achieve that number by enrolling a smaller number of higher-caliber students who would take a larger academic load. We knew that goal would require an intense recruiting effort with special attention to diversity and the judicious use of what scholarship funds we had available. That plan, however, ran against the grain of an emerging trend.

MDiv enrollment demonstrated this trend. In the 1980s the seminary's MDiv enrollment remained in the 200s. Those students registered for about 5,000 tuition hours for an average of about 22.3 hours per student. By the late 1990s we enrolled more than 300 MDiv students, but they registered for only 5,200 hours or about 16.7 hours per student. That meant we had to admit more students to achieve the same number of hours.

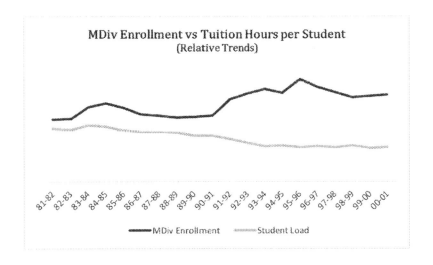

The chart shows trend lines. The actual numbers show MDiv total enrollment (upper line) increasing from 223 to 311, while the average tuition hours per MDiv student (lower line) dropped from 22.3 to 16.7 during the same span of time.

The message: We continually needed more students to generate the same tuition revenue.

The cause of that trend lay in the social changes taking place. Candidates for the ministry, generally speaking, had become older. They had families, they had jobs, and they had less time for study. They also had economic pressure from the rising cost of tuition, which led to their need to borrow more money. Even the primary source of our additional MDiv students—African-American and Caucasian women—mirrored this trend. But they too tended to be middle-age working adults.

Programs

Clearly, then, the seminary's financial well-being called for us to attract a greater number of students. The increased competition from other seminaries, including four new seminary programs in our backyard, produced a challenge requiring innovative solutions, such as new programs.

Traditionally, 70-75 percent of Wesley's tuition hours came from the Master of Divinity (MDiv) program. The Doctor of Ministry program (DMin), which offered continuing education and professional enhancement for pastors already in ministry, had produced less than 8 percent of the tuition hours. Then, because of the changing nature of the student body and the rising cost of education, we began to shift attention toward the DMin program during the late 1980s. We urged the faculty to create a program which addressed the special interests and needs of pastors, including time flexibility in course offerings.

They came up with a model designed around specialty tracks of particular interest such as leadership excellence. Five or six tracks were available with two or three new ones beginning each year. Each track offered six required courses and two electives. Each required course was offered as a one-week intensive, available during a period of two weeks in January and a similar period in the summer.

The two electives could be taken online, by directed study, or in some other program of choice. To fulfill requirements for the DMin degree, each candidate also completed an in-ministry project that was submitted in written form to an examining committee.

Enrollment in the DMin program exploded—an increase of almost 350 percent from 1990-1998. The entrepreneurial skills of Kyunglim Shin Lee proved essential. She brought DMin candidates in from Korea and other countries. Eventually, the program extended outward from the Wesley campus to include other communities in the United States, Europe, and Asia.

Even though our DMin enrollment grew dramatically, it remained a small portion of our tuition income—about 14 percent at best. The expansion of this program, however, was more cost-effective because we could employ Wesley's faculty—already on the payroll. The participation of a large number of geographically-diverse pastors, who sang our praises around the world, created enormous good will and visibility for Wesley. Many of them also recommend younger students for our MDiv program.

The following chart illustrates the DMin program's wide acceptance.

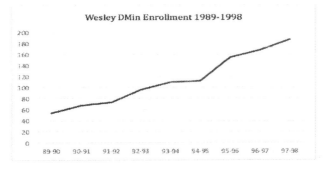

Wesley DMin Enrollment 1989-1998

Wesley was not the only seminary pushing the DMin, so what made ours so well received? The answer most likely can be found within this list of key elements:

- Offering tracks geared to the special interests and needs of pastors
- Participating with a group of colleagues who remained together through the core courses and became a supportive learning group
- Focus upon an educational experience that would enhance pastoral skills
- Offerings within time frames convenient for pastors.
- Interactive courses designed by Wesley faculty, drawing on ideas and experiences of the participating pastors
- Some church agencies and other schools providing special learning resources that enhanced particular tracks
- International immersion experience offered in some tracks
- Opportunity for participants to spend time in Washington, D.C.

Faculty

From the outset of my tenure, I had appreciated the faculty for their unswerving dedication to the mission of Wesley Seminary. During this dynamic period of the late 90s, they doubled down their contribution by injecting fresh energy into our new and expanded programs. They took on extra work loads to accommodate the DMin program expansion. They adjusted to new methods of preparation and teaching styles the DMin required. They learned from the pastors in this new program, which in turned positively affected their teaching in MDiv courses.

Many of them also invested in the development and the teaching of lay education courses that became part of the Wesley Ministry Network, which provided a curriculum for congregations.

The seminary's dramatic growth in programs and student numbers had indeed created new demands on the faculty. The significant increase in the number of students created extra-large enrollments in the core-required courses. In order to reduce classroom sizes and thus provide more opportunity for personal interaction between teacher and students, the Wesley faculty voluntarily taught two sections of each intro course. The influx of new students increased the time that all of the faculty members spent counseling and advising.

To better serve students with full-time jobs, the faculty agreed to offer degree courses during Friday evenings and Saturdays for the first time ever. The seminary had come a long way from the 1980s, when some faculty members had refused even to consider teaching evening courses.

Faculty Compensation

Wesley had a policy of equal salary for every faculty member in the same rank, and the same annual percentage raise regardless of rank. As a result, our senior faculty members began to lag behind their counterparts at comparable seminaries. The faculty as a whole suggested that we modify the policy and provide senior members a larger percentage of increase for the next three years. The board gave strong approval to that idea.

The board also allocated an annual $50,000 fund dedicated to encouraging and enabling faculty research. A faculty member could apply for a grant from the fund to support a particular research project. That positively affected faculty morale.

In recognition of the increasing cost of housing in the Washington area, the board expanded its housing support policy for newly-arriving members of the faculty. They could now receive a second mortgage up to one-third the value of their house to a maximum of $75,000. They need only pay interest on the loan for the first 10 years. Further assistance came in the form of a $6,000 grant to defray the cost of closing and settlement.

Finally we provided added compensation for faculty members teaching each DMin course and supervising a project thesis.

The President's Role

In the early days of my tenure, I assumed—as did everyone else—that fundraising was and would continue to be the key to the seminary's fiscal well-being. That suited me because I could raise money, and I liked doing it. But later, as I settled into the job and saw that tuition brought in three times as much as fundraising, I re-evaluated my role. The question became how a goal-directed, action-oriented president could best influence the critical level of enrollment.

The answer came slowly, with experience: I should not be making rounds of the colleges and talking with every potential student who showed up. My job would be to create a system, assemble the right component parts, and make sure those parts worked smoothly and effectively. In other words, I was supposed to lead the orchestra, not play the cello.

Once I accepted that role, I discovered several items in need of attention:

- Did we have an effective admissions staff that regularly contacted and positively influenced prospective students to attend Wesley?
- Did they have adequate resources to do the job?
- Did the seminary have scholarship resources that would attract and assist students to enroll in its programs?
- Did the seminary have the kind of faculty and programs that would attract students?
- Did the faculty, where possible, support and engage with prospective students and work to retain those already enrolled?
- Did we have a campus with educational, worship, community, and living facilities that would attract students and provide a compelling experience while they were attending?
- Was Wesley visible and admired in our region, nationally, and internationally in a fashion that would influence students to choose Wesley?
- Was the board attuned to the complexity and systemic nature of producing and maintaining an adequate number of quality students? Merely reporting enrollment statistics to them was not enough.

With all that to keep track of, I no longer questioned what I should be doing. I needed to focus on the institutional overview—visioning, planning, and facilitating—and to provide the resources needed to help us achieve it.

VIII. Facilities

In the early Christian church, monasteries became the primary location for education and formation of those who would lead the church's ministries. Their education model was built around a community life of worship, education, work, and discipline. They believed the necessary facilities included a chapel, library, teaching space, refectory, and living quarters. Those components of an educational community have continued over the generations and are still evident in most theological schools. Although developments in telecommunications have begun to alter that model, some forms of face-to-face learning are still considered to be the gold standard.

From the very outset of my presidency, I continually grappled with educational settings and spaces. In 1995 we conducted a study with three objectives: (1) review all campus spaces and how they were being used; (2) identify needs for improvements and for additional space; and (3) identify undeveloped and underutilized areas and determine how to bring them into use.

Basically, we needed space for offices, classrooms, and residence halls. We were short in every category. We had already begun to put faculty offices into the single-students' dormitory rooms (Straughn Hall). Built during the late 1950s, it was as sturdy as a bomb shelter. That made it nearly impossible to move walls or change the communal bathrooms. Renovation would cost $6.2 million, but it didn't stop there. The building had no air-conditioning and we could install only a few window units because of electric power limitations. Correcting that problem alone would require a major, campus-wide infrastructure upgrade that would cost another $4 million. Reluctantly, we had to postpone the dormitory upgrade and power enhancement.

We were able to renovate some underutilized space in the basement of Straughn Hall, which allowed us to move the Church's Center for Theology and Public Policy out of the Trott administration building. Some opposed the move, implying the president did not value Wesley's long-standing commitment to theology and public policy. I took the heat for that decision.

254

That decision nevertheless enabled us to relocate our growing staff and program in student recruitment and admissions into the expanded, upgraded space in the Trott building. Inasmuch as that was directly above the president's office, the admissions staff enjoyed proclaiming themselves as being "above the president."

As the seminary's enrollment increased, we ran short of adequate classroom space for larger introductory courses required for incoming students. Young Whan Park, an architect and member of the board, came to the rescue. He conceived a new design combining two inadequate classrooms into a larger, semi-circular, four-tiered lecture hall with 100+ seating capacity. It was equipped with the latest technology and could be adapted for special events such as dramatic productions. The board approved $250,000 thousand for that project, which virtually transformed much of Wesley's education program.

During the process of evaluating space utilization, we recognized that electronic data processing had become essential not only as a tool for the seminary's requirements but as part of the education program itself. Our first major step in that direction was an office-and-classroom LAN connection. With tech support included, the cost exceeded $1 million. However, that provided access to students as well as staff and set us on track for online education.

Reluctant Postponement

Although the board approved the major investments in IT and classroom renovation, several other needs had to be deferred to the next administration because of financial limitations and other educational priorities. I was nevertheless proud to realize those functional improvements also made the campus more esthetically

255

appealing and seemed to boost the morale of our whole community.

Later, I became even prouder of the next administration. They developed a bold plan that addressed all the needs we had been forced to postpone—a major upgrade of the infrastructure, renovation of the library and chapel, and construction of a beautiful new dormitory.

IX. Finance

In financial planning, the temptation is to think short term. Some schools allow themselves to dip into multi-year grant monies to solve immediate problems. They fully intend to restore those funds, but the next year brings a new set of problems and the loan is never repaid. Some managers develop the habit of using unrestricted endowment funds like an interest-free credit card with no payback required. That practice had earlier led Wesley Seminary to the brink of financial ruin.

During the early period of my tenure, I was lured ever so close to those same treacherous shoals. With the seminary struggling to stay afloat, the task of balancing the budget made it difficult to think of the future. We worked hard to balance the budget four consecutive years and pay off the endowment loans. Only then, when it finally appeared that we were going to survive, could we lift our eyes to the far horizon. The days of living hand-to-mouth had passed.

As we then began to plan ahead, I realized we had to match budgets with goals. We had to be certain that resources were available to sustain us through fulfillment of our plans. We had to design a long-term financial strategy that would include investments in our physical plant as well as enhancing our education programs, faculty, and staff. There seemed to be an endless list of things we needed to do.

Gradually, I became more financially astute and began to plan for a more distant future.

Two successful capital campaigns had raised our morale, given us more confidence, and provided us with a reasonable measure of financial flexibility. By 1995 we stood poised to make another forward leap programmatically as well as financially.

Financial Realities—Some Hard Choices

In spite of our successes, all was not flawless. Our annual fundraising program had leveled off except for minor increases, and even those were outpaced by the cost of living. Our endowment remained small at $12 million. Tuition hours were still the primary income generator, and we kept shifting that load onto the backs of the students. Our campus infrastructure and facilities needed additional investment. Information technology—the new kid on the block—demanded a fresh infusion of money to bring Wesley into the modern technological world.

Our joint planning committee—made up of board members, administration, faculty, and staff—had been wrestling with those realities for more than a year. Finally, we recommended a three-fold strategy: creation of a new strategic plan, a capital campaign, and a 10-year financial plan.

Ten-Year Financial Plan

No one can see 10 years into the future. Our charge in 1997, nevertheless, was to set a course that would prepare Wesley Seminary to negotiate the challenges of a new century looming straight ahead. Determined efforts, with help from the newly-developed spreadsheet technology, allowed us to project numbers forward in order to anticipate the most likely problem areas. We generated a 10-year plan with guidelines that would require annual assessment of critical areas followed by adjustments that would enable us to hold the long-range course.

We divided the plan into three parts: operating income, operating expenses, and capital income and expense. Operating income was the most critical. Everything else depended on that.

Operating Income

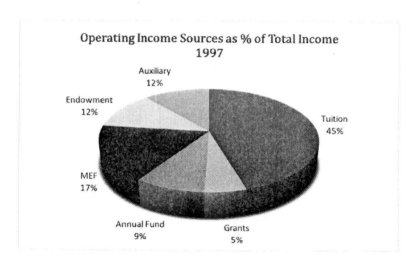

Tuition. We projected masters degree hours at 7,600 annually and DMin at 1,000, which meant maintaining our enrollment at its current level. Given the size of our faculty and facilities, we planned to hold the total hours to 8,600.

We had increased tuition 5 percent each year for the past 15 years, which resulted in a dramatic increase of over 200 percent in that span of time. For the sake of our students, we wanted to restrain those increases, even though tuition remained our number one source of income. Reluctantly, we decided on a transition: continue the 5 percent increase for three more years, reduce it to 4 percent for the next two years, and thereafter keep it stabilized at 3 percent. Tuition would still remain about 44 percent of our operating income.

Grants. This source had been growing steadily as a result of our aggressive efforts. We projected a 4 percent annual increase, which would bring it up to 6 percent of operating income.

Annual Fund. This, we assumed, would continue its steady but modest growth of 3 percent, producing about 9 percent of operating income.

MEF. Although the United Methodist Church Ministerial Educational Fund was a critical component of the seminary's income budget, it had been slipping. We assumed no more than a 1 percent annual increase from that source. It would decline from 17 percent to 13 percent of income during the ten-year life of the plan.

Endowment. For 15 years, Wesley had been robbing Peter to pay Paul by dipping too deeply into its pool of endowment funds to access operational money. That had to stop. Even after curbing the double-digit draw rate from the early 1980s, we continued to violate the 5 percent rule of thumb. While already drawing 7 percent from the fund in the late eighties, we took another 3.5 percent to support a capital campaign. That meant we were siphoning off 10.5 percent of the endowment every year. (I was a bit naive in those earlier years regarding endowment management and withdrawal rates, as were most of our board members.)

By 1995-96 we had reduced our draw rate to 6 percent, which produced $752,000 for the operation budget in 1997. We then made two risky moves. First, in the ten-year plan we set the draw from endowment at 6 percent, plus an additional $70,000 draw every year for ten years. Second, we proposed to cover that additional draw with a commitment to raise at least $1.4 million dollars for the endowment every year. For that plan to work, we would need to double our endowment within the next 10 years. It was a big, bold risk. If we were successful, endowment would leap from 12 percent to 17 percent of income.

Some board members were uncomfortable with that proposal. They suggested the draw rate be reduced to a more prudent 5 percent by 2000. They knew our strategy was risky, but we pressed for it because we needed a breakout in our endowment income. The board finally approved the plan.

Auxiliary. We planned to increase auxiliary and other income at a 3 percent rate.

Our total operating income for fiscal 1997 was $6,311,660. If the plan worked perfectly, the seminary would end fiscal 2006 with an operating income of $8,568,94—and a balanced budget.

Operating Expenses

We based our estimate of expense increases on the federal government's projection of the cost of living and inflation.

Income Source	Fiscal Yr 1997	% of Income	Annual Increase	Fiscal Yr 2006	% of Income
Tuition	2,861,994	45%	Avg. 3.8%	3,757,925	44%
Grants	326,136	5%	4%	547,377	6%
Annual Fund	556,000	9%	3%	750,181	9%
MEF	1,094,000	17%	1%	1,126,000	13%
Endow	752,300	12%	$70K/Year	1,465,300	17%
Auxiliary	721,330	12%	3%	922,158	11%
Total	6,311,670			8,568,941	

We assumed the low end of those predictions and therefore increased all expense lines by 3 percent for the life of the plan, with one exception: scholarship aid was pegged to the rate of tuition increase.

Fiscal 1996-97 was a good year for the seminary. Expenses came to $5,909,254, which left the operations fund with a healthy net of $402,406.

Our 10-year projection, based on our income and expense assumptions, did not always point to a balanced operational budget. In fact, we forecast five deficit years out of the coming 10. Those were warning signals that would force us to seek alternative strategies in the future.

Capital Income and Expense

The search for expense money for capital improvements and other special needs over and above the regular building and grounds budgets had been a continuing challenge during my entire tenure. It became no easier in the 10-year plan.

We decided first to commit all undesignated bequests to the capital improvements fund. Bequests had averaged about $130,000 per year. We had planned to increase that by $5,000 per year. However, that would leave us well short of the estimated annual need of $450,000 for capital expense. We had to find some way to make up the difference.

Early in the capital campaign we received a special gift of $1 million to upgrade our information technology capacity. We spread the use of that gift over five years at $200,000 per year. We then made yet another risky decision by planning to use $500,000 each year for four years in the annual operating budget from "the yet to be raised" capital campaign. With those two additions, the total net operations would project a balanced budget for the seminary through 2002. Beyond that point, we showed an overall deficit in net operations until achieving a modest surplus in the final year of the plan.

A Delicate Financial Future

By 1997, Wesley was in the strongest financial condition in its history. However, not all of its problems were solved. We still needed a successful capital campaign in order to fulfill our strategic plan and guarantee a sustainable financial future. The plan required us to increase our endowment significantly—actually double it.

All too often, the gods of finance seem to give, then take away. The capital campaign surpassed our wildest dreams—more than $30 million raised by 2001. The historic bull market of the 1990s also had a dramatic effect. From 1995 to 2000, Wesley's investment portfolio increased by 250 percent to a total of more than $32 million. We had more than doubled our $12 million endowment in just five years.

The gods reversed that trend with a 25 percent market decline over the next three years. The terrorist attack of 9/11 then created anxiety and loss of direction for many individuals and institutions.

Wesley Seminary weathered the 21st century fiscal storm, but was reminded that all plans, whether short or long, can be dramatically altered by events outside of its control. During our two-decade climb to fiscal health and stability, we faced many ups and downs. We discovered the necessity of focusing on the seminary's mission, thoughtful planning, and openness to change, and flexibility in the face of unexpected challenges.

Continuing Concerns

I never rested easily, even as we scaled ever-higher financial mountains. There always seemed to be greater needs and loftier dreams crying for attention along with the ever-present pressure to achieve annual targets. The road to financial sustainability had no end:

- There never seemed to be enough scholarship money to meet student needs, to attract students with great potential, or just to meet our income quota of tuition hours

- The needs of a physical plant and investments in new educational resources were insatiable

- Every year, the wish to affirm our dedicated faculty and staff with tangible support for their hard work lay heavy on my heart

Wrestling with these ever-present concerns, I never felt more like a father with an utterly dependent family whose daily and long-term needs relied on my leadership, my daily productivity. Rationally, I knew I could not achieve this miracle alone, but I never escaped feeling responsible for it.

Leadership and Change: A President's Story

Phase V

Transition and Beyond

2000-2002

Leaving the Party

I began my 18th year as president of Wesley Seminary on the first of July, 1999, and turned 65 later that summer. My health was excellent. I had tons of energy, and my job still filled me with excitement. But in the back of my mind I could hear my mother's old saying: "You should always leave the party while you are having a good time."

That was easier said than done. I had seen Wesley come a long way during my tenure, and I had dedicated myself to ensuring that its future would be a bright one. But there was no way to get around the fact that transition of presidential leadership at any institution is bound to have a significant effect—one way or another. It was a critical time.

For Wesley, it was also a busy time. We were in the midst of the largest capital campaign the seminary had ever undertaken. I had promised to remain in office at least through the completion of that, which would come at the end of June, 2001. The board, however, would need sufficient advance notice if they were to work out plans for a smooth transition. With that in mind, I shared my thoughts with some of leaders of the board and the campaign. We decided to raise the issue formally with the board's executive committee during its meeting in December of 1999.

We received less than a pleasant reaction. Many of the board members insisted that I should not be thinking of retirement yet. Wesley, after all, was on a roll: the campaign was going well, enrollment was strong, and the seminary's reputation had never been better. They said I still had lots of get up and go, so why should I consider retirement at that particular moment? I stressed again the need for planning to ensure continuation of that success. Some committee members felt it was unnecessary—downright inappropriate—to talk about succession until a firm date for retirement had been set.

Board Meeting: February 2000

I had some reservations and feelings of anxiety. The job, after all, had become central to my identity. I persisted in discussions with leaders of the board nonetheless. The chair of the board and I decided and then, acting jointly, raised the issue before the full board in executive session. It was the first time they had received formal notice. Many of them expressed concerns similar to those of the executive committee—primarily the risk of jeopardizing the ongoing financial campaign. They were also concerned about maintaining the clear direction that Wesley had developed in its strategic plan, which was now underway and looking better all the time.

A frank and lengthy discussion resulted in the board's request that I continue to serve as president at least until July of 2002. That would provide a full year of transition following completion of the capital campaign. I agreed to their request.

Successor

Enter David McAllister-Wilson. He and I had been close colleagues and friends for 18 years. His natural talent and leadership skills had matured wonderfully well during that time. I knew of his calling and his desire, and I knew without question that he would make an excellent president for any seminary fortunate enough to recruit him. That was not my judgment alone. David had gained wide respect from the entire Wesley community. His leadership potential was common knowledge to other United Methodist theological schools as well. Several of them, in fact, were actively searching for a new president and had his name on their short lists. One of them had already contacted him. It was almost a foregone conclusion that David would be offered a presidency before the end of the year.

Although I was certain that David was the ideal choice to succeed me at Wesley, I was careful not to lobby for him with the board, even privately. He needed to be recruited and selected on his own merits. Open advocacy on my part might well have undercut his credibility. That made it delicate for me to respond to the numerous inquiries about him that came from other schools. I did not hesitate to provide a strong endorsement, but I did not want him to leave. I felt like someone walking a tightrope.

I made it a point not to discuss my retirement thoughts with David, or his potential as president of Wesley or any other seminary. He in turn kept to himself about those matters. Both of us were fully aware of the ongoing dynamics. He knew how dear Wesley was to my heart, and he knew that I was willing to trust him with its future. After all our time together, further talk or speculation or strategizing would be fruitless and possibly complicate the situation. We said nothing.

Executive Committee Meeting: April 2000

Following the February board meeting, there was a buzz among the members about a presidential transition. They had finally accepted that I would indeed be retiring before long. In April, the executive committee met in executive session—no staff present—to discuss the issue of presidential transition. The atmosphere crackled with ideas and strongly-held opinions on transition matters great and small. What kind of person could best lead Wesley Seminary into the 21st century? How should the selection process be handled? When should it begin?

Some committee members worried that David McAllister-Wilson might be lost to some other seminary. Others believed that his capabilities would be enhanced by experience gained at the helm of another institution. That notion brought up the question of how Wesley could get him back if he were to leave. Yet another faction posed the possibility of introducing a "fresh perspective" by bringing in someone from the outside. Consideration of an "outside" selection pointed toward a national search. Comparison to other candidates might well put David into a stronger position. Or not. But wait: shouldn't the board consult the faculty and other support groups too before proceeding?

Tradition had developed into a policy that dictated an open search for any vacant position at the seminary, especially the presidency. Supporters of that idea held a strong hand; they advocated the need to consider a diversity of candidates.

Another tradition, unspoken but widely pervasive, held that when discussions become extended, candid, and heated, yet fail to produce a consensus, it is time to set up a committee. That is what the executive committee did. They established a transition committee charged with answering three questions: (1) should an outside consultant be called in to assist in the search; (2) should the search be internal or external; and (3) who should be involved in the search? The board chair and the president would decide how best to keep the Wesley community informed of decisions and progress.

Full Board Meeting: May 2000

After dispensing with the usual business items in the morning session, the board dedicated the afternoon to an executive session. I was present as an ex-officio member, but I was determined not to speak unless asked a direct question. I wanted the board to exercise its responsibility by choosing the next president without my intervening in any way.

An amazing and totally unpredictable process evolved. The chair of the board began by reporting on the executive committee's meeting and its recommendation to set up a transition committee. He then announced there would be a national search for a new president. That drew an immediate, emotional response from several board members. They not only questioned the wisdom of such an action; they insisted that a national search had not been one of the executive committee's recommendations. Edward Hoerr, a board member who had served on several search committees in other institutions, said, "Let me tell you about national searches. They may sound right in principle, but they do not always produce good results. Why should we hope to find some ideal candidate when we already have an outstanding candidate right in our midst—someone we all know and trust."

A number of board members nodded heads in agreement.

The board chair, somewhat taken aback, gathered himself and said he had obviously misread the board's feelings. He then made an unusual but brilliant proposal. He asked that each board member speak in turn, candidly expressing his or her feelings regarding the matter and how we should proceed.

270

After a few moments of silence, the most dramatic group process that I had ever witnessed began to unfold. There were some 30 board members present. Everyone took a turn. Some spoke for several minutes, while others merely offered a sentence of agreement, but the timbre of emotion resonated within each voice. Twice during the sharing a member asked that the group pause for a moment of prayer. With various words and images they asked for insight, wisdom, and courage.

An hour later, when the last member had spoken, it was absolutely clear that David McAllister-Wilson would be the next president of Wesley Seminary.

In the wake of that remarkable event, they asked for my opinion. Was David the best person for the job? I said that if a better candidate did exist, I didn't know who it might be. I told them I had known many seminary presidents from one end of the country to the other, and not a single one would I rank ahead of the person they had chosen to lead Wesley into the future.

The board members recognized the seminary community's consensus about the direction of the seminary that had emerged from a decade of work. No one wanted to risk disrupting this clarity. Bringing in a new president, no matter how qualified risked derailing the seminary's current trajectory.

Members also realized that finding an excellent candidate for a seminary presidency was not easy or guaranteed. Many feared that we might lose David in the process.

Someone moved that David McAllister-Wilson be affirmed as the board of governors' candidate for the

271

next president of Wesley Seminary. The board would then consult with other key groups in the Wesley community, including staff, students, graduates, church constituency, and especially the faculty. If they heard strong support for David, the board would then officially elect him to be the next president. The motion passed unanimously.

Sharing with David

The board officers and I were instructed to meet with David, report on the board's action, relate the board's strong affirmation of him, and ask if he would accept this proposal and process. David, at first astounded, recovered quickly and said yes. He then added that he had never really wanted to be president of just any seminary. He felt that his calling had always been to Wesley.

After the board officers left, David and I sat there trying to take it all in. He said, "I can't believe this is happening." When I told him how the meeting had progressed, and what tremendous respect they had shown for him and how confident they felt about their choice, he said it again—several times. It was a good day for both of us.

Later, I sat alone reflecting on the drama of the day and on the evolution of the Wesley board during the past two decades. I was proud of the board, not just because members had chosen David, but because they recognized their responsibility and had the courage to act on it. They demonstrated two critical functions of a good board. They were very clear about the mission and direction of the seminary and would not alter the course.

They were also committed to securing leadership that shared that vision and who had to capacity to lead the seminary on its chosen path into the 21st century. They knew they had compromised somewhat on their principles and policies, but they decided that mission and leadership trumped.

Even as I contemplated their merits that day, I had yet to realize the full strength of that board. When their action became public, it gave rise to an angry opposition, particularly from members of the faculty. In the face of this anger and opposition, the board held its ground, never wavering.

What a day it had been!

Summer 2000

In early June the board leadership had a tumultuous meeting with the entire faculty. Quite a few of the faculty members were upset. They claimed the board had violated accepted seminary procedures for choosing a president. Most especially, they had gone against the seminary's affirmative action policies. Moreover, the faculty had been given no say-so the process and were neither consulted nor informed beforehand.

The board members countered by insisting that its action was not an election. They were now consulting everyone with regard to their preferred candidate. Furthermore, they had not violated seminary policy: the bylaws clearly state it is the responsibility and obligation of the board to select the president, and the bylaws do not prescribe how that is done. The board is free to invite any person or any group it deems necessary to participate in the selection process—or none, if it so chooses.

On those issues, the board leadership met several more times with a committee from the faculty. They also consulted church leaders and met with groups of staff, students, and members of the graduates' association. Those events produced three interesting results.

First: The faculty invited David to its annual fall retreat for an extended discussion. (I felt that I should not attend.) When it was over, they chose to support David as Wesley's next president. The vote was unanimous.

Second: In February of 2001, the faculty, staff, and board held a retreat focused on authority, governance, and decision-making. They approached those topics through Bible study and theological reflection as background for discussion about the seminary's policies and practices regarding authority and governance, both present and future. That retreat proved to be a very healing event.

Third: Perhaps the most conflicted issue generated by the board's decision had to do with affirmative action policies. They stated that each search should be open, seeking internal and external candidates, especially ethnic minorities and women.

In October of 2000, the board formally elected David as president, effective upon my retirement on July 1, 2002.

Life in the Transition Lane

Having a president-elect on the premises for almost two years before taking office is unusual, to say the least. That sort of arrangement is occasionally used in the business world, but is rare in the field of education. If it is to work out well, the two individuals must have confidence and trust each other.

As colleagues of long standing, David and I had no trouble whatsoever, and the board was perfectly comfortable. I retained the responsibilities and authority of the president, and the Wesley community continued to respond to me in that way. David and I took care to avoid being pitted against each other, and we always put our heads together before reaching important decisions. Gradually, the mantle of leadership began to shift toward him as people looked upon him as their leader of the future.

I continued to focus on fundraising for the capital campaign and promoting the seminary locally, nationally, and internationally. The latter function took me to Korea for an immersion trip with faculty and students, then to Hawaii to carry out development work in Korean churches under the guidance of Kyunglim Shin Lee.

In the summer of 2001, Shirley and I took our final study leave in Cambridge. That setting provided the opportunity to gear up for the coming year and reflect on the ending of a journey that had lasted two decades and brought an inexpressible wealth of experience and meaning into our lives.

The ongoing search for new faculty and senior staff continued without letup. Our vice president for finance had left for a new opportunity. Filling that senior position became a top priority. Whoever we chose would be working closely with the future president, so I made a point of seeing that David played a key role in the selection process. It was he, in fact, who found the candidate who was elected to the position.

David and I, along with Dean Bruce Birch, spent considerable time working on the academic program. Although David had very little experience in that area, he and Bruce formed an effective partnership that would serve the seminary's academic program well. Bruce and I saw to it that David became an integral part of the search for key faculty members.

A Growing Leadership Role

David took on many more responsibilities during those last two years. The capital campaign, the new Lilly grant, the strategic plan, the 10-year financial plan—they were all going to be under his guidance, not to mention the numerous daily management details of an educational institution in full swing. He had been instrumental in launching many of those initiatives, so his assumption of leadership was a natural progression. From day one, he was a driving force behind Wesley's partnership with churches in developing congregational partners, a Culture of the Call campaign , and Wesley's programmatic efforts in the four annual conferences. The Wesley Ministry Network, which created educational materials for local churches and continuing education for pastors, was his idea. David also set his sights on the next stage of strategic planning as he began laying the groundwork for new program initiatives and a master plan for the campus.

I felt reasonably comfortable with the transition. It was moving along with great success and it was the right thing to do—rationally.

Emotionally, I felt occasional twinges of regret. I had always enjoyed being in the center of the action, the one in control of what was to happen, and the one responsible for the outcome. Now I had to keep reminding myself that I had chosen to relinquish the power and influence of a chief executive.

There was, I suppose, something universal about that feeling of regret: all good things must come to an end. But that doesn't mean it will be painless.

An apparently innocuous event, in a way, seemed, for me, to symbolize the passing of the torch. Mike Kelley had taken over as chair of the governing board. He had supported David's election, and now they had become the spearhead for Wesley's future. Mike came into my office one morning and greeted me with a cheerful "Hi, Doug." Without pausing, he proceeded onward into David's office and closed the door behind him. The two proceeded to strategize about the future of the seminary. I was left on the outside, wishing I was on the inside.

David probably knew the same thing, maybe even before I did, but he handled the situation extraordinarily well. He never overstepped any boundaries. He always made me feel I was a valued colleague, mentor, friend, and the president.

Longevity and Continuity

As previously mentioned, transition of presidential leadership can become a diversion serious enough to knock the clarity of mission out of focus and affect the confidence of supporters. Building a constituency is a long-term process, and confidence in the top leadership is critical. Wesley Seminary, I think, was fortunate to have longevity in its senior leadership and continuity in leadership succession that confirmed and sustained its mission and direction.

Saying Goodbye

Very few people enjoy goodbyes. I certainly do not. I tried to avoid it, on campus and off, but that was impossible. I was thanked by many in various ways, and I was deeply appreciative of each one. Some people cried, and I almost did too on a couple of occasions. I received a considerable number of letters. They were placed in a handcrafted box and presented to me at a Wesley community lunch in my honor. I decided not to read the letters right away—too much buzzing through my head already. I read them a year later, and they touched my heart. They also gave me further insight into how I was perceived as a person as well as a leader.

The board of governors gave a dinner for Shirley and me at a local country club. It was a marvelous event with speeches about what a great president I had been. I can scarcely remember what was said. I do remember making the rounds of the tables to offer thanks to all the guests. The memory of sharing so much of my life with those people, growing and changing with them, caring for them and having them care for me in return—that is still within my heart and my soul and will forever remain.

Neither Wesley Seminary nor I would ever be the same because of what we all did together for twenty years. Thanks be to God.

After leaving office, I did not return but once or twice during the following year, although our new house is only five blocks away. I have made it a practice not to give advice to the seminary or to David unless I am specifically asked for it. David and I remain close friends. We often talk about the seminary, but I always want it to be at his initiative. I have also continued to stay in touch with and occasionally visit Wesley supporters whose primary connection to the seminary was through me. At the seminary's invitation I have served on the advisory board of the Lewis Leadership Center and one committee of the board of governors.

My primary role has been external cheerleader and advocate for Wesley Seminary.

Beyond Wesley

In spite of being a planner by nature, I deliberately had not set many specific goals for retirement. I wanted the freedom of choosing from whatever opportunities might come my way. The first opportunity came within a week, when the doctor told me I had prostate cancer and I had the freedom to choose the treatment. That was not a welcome retirement gift.

I took the surgical option. Thankfully, it turned out to be the right choice because five months later I was free of the cancer, and new opportunities to continue my work in theological education surfaced.

From the very outset of my presidency, I promoted the idea of leadership in the church. I even encouraged the seminary to establish a Center for Church Leadership. Leadership became an increasing part of our conversations and our programs, but no center emerged. The year of my retirement, unbeknownst to me, the Wesley Governing Board established just such a center. They raised a million dollars to launch it, and named it the G. Douglass Lewis Center for Church Leadership. I was stunned, but delighted. Lovett Weems, who was ready to step down as president of St. Paul School of Theology, accepted the job as the first director. After 17 years, the "fearsome threesome" of the early 1980s was reunited. Under Lovett's direction, the Center has become enormously successful in helping pastors and congregations become more effective leaders in the church's ministries. I am immensely proud of the accomplishments of the Center and the creative leadership of Lovett Weems and David McAllister-Wilson.

Sometimes good things do come to those who wait.

Dan Aleshire, executive director of the Association of Theological Schools, asked if I would be interested in helping design a new program for seminary presidents, and then serve as its first dean. We developed a week intensive on issues and skills needed to be an effective seminary president. I served in that capacity for six years and got to know dozens of seminary presidents from across North America. Based on that experience, we published A Handbook for Seminary Presidents that led me into consulting with many more presidents during the ensuing decade.

The staff of the Religion Division of Lilly Endowment asked me to do a follow-up research project related to one of their major grant programs. That opened the door to several other opportunities to work with the Endowment's grant programs for theological schools.

In Trust, with its program focusing on seminary boards and governance, asked me to serve on its board and then become chair for several years. Ultimately they asked me to serve as acting president and create a proposal to Lilly Endowment to reshape the organization into the In Trust Center for Theological Schools with the objective of helping schools identify and utilize resources to increase their effectiveness.

My family always said I was a theological education junkie. They were right. More than a decade into retirement, I still found myself privileged to work with dozens of seminaries and their leaders here and abroad. I kept learning from them.

These small educational institutions have a more pervasive impact on the church and society than their size would appear to warrant. They shape hundreds of individuals whose leadership in turn affects countless individuals, churches, and other organizations without whom our world would be less caring, compassionate, and meaningful.

What a gift I received—becoming a part of that extended community of formation and service we call theological education. My call many years ago felt right. No one could possibly ask for a better opportunity to live it out.